Dr. Steph

Legacy
RELOADED
A Nonviolent Awakening

Chosen Pen Publishing

ISBN Paperback: 978-1-952315-64-0

Library Congress of Control Number:

10 9 8 7 6 5 4 3 2 1

To order additional copies of the resource, write Chosen Pen Customer Service:1420 Hoke Loop Road Fayetteville, NC 28314 FAX orders to 910-868-3300 Phone orders to 910-818-6652

Website: www.chosepen.com
www.chosenpenacademy.com

Printed in the United States of America

Contents

Dedication

Foreword

Introduction   3

39   10

Chapter 1

A Child of God   15

In Pursuit of Purpose   23

Chapter 2

Retracing the Journey of a King   27
Restoring Peace by Embracing Dr. King's Principles of

Nonviolence   33

Chapter 3

Imprints of Time   37

Introspection   43

Chapter 4

In the Footprints of Heroes   47

Taking Charge of Change   61

Chapter 5

Get Off My Shoulders   63

Peace as Currency   72

Chapter 6

Where Do We Go from Here   75

A Perspective Born from Knowledge   85

Chapter 7

An Ordinary Man's Extraordinary Faith   89

The Turning Point   106

Chapter 8

The March That Changed America   109

Stepping into Greatness Channeling Dr. King's Legacy 121

Chapter 9

Bridging Generations   123

A Call to Contemplate Our Impact   131

Chapter 10

Democracy's Fragile Chain is the Missing Vote   133

An Intimate Glimpse of Dr. King   137

Chapter 11

Revelatory Reflections and Narratives That Influence 139

Chapter 12

Something To Consider   143

TheDreamLives.com   157

Acknowledgments

About the Author

Dedication

Legacy Reloaded is lovingly dedicated to my cherished ninety-two-year-old mother, Parthenia Ferguson, and in fond remembrance of my father, Elzabad Ferguson, Sr. It is dedicated to my beautiful daughter, Iyanna Dajé Ferguson, and my eleven siblings and their families, whose support and love are my foundation. In a heartfelt tribute, I also dedicate this work to the dear family members we have lost: my sisters Damaris Rozelda Jackson and Marcia Lanese Ferguson, my brother Deonesus Andrew Ferguson, and my nephews Harold James Ferguson Jr. (J.R.), Elzabad Helon Ferguson Jr. (Chaz), and niece April Johnson.

Legacy Reloaded honors the enduring friendships and invaluable support of long-time friends who have been pivotal in shaping my journey and work with Dr. King. To Aurelia C. Mclean, James A. Marshall Jr., Herbert Miller, Electa Person, and Joe McGee, your influence and assistance have been instrumental in bringing this endeavor to fruition.

My spiritual growth came with the guidance of Bishop Reverend Dr. Brian R. Thompson, Reverend Dr. Allen McLaughlin, and Reverend Dr. William E. Flippin Sr.

Most importantly, I dedicate Legacy Reloaded to my Father, God.

"Sooner or later all the people of the world will have to discover a way to live together in peace, and thereby transform this pending cosmic elegy into a creative psalm of brotherhood. If this is to be achieved, man must evolve for all human conflict a method which rejects revenge, aggression, and retaliation. The foundation of such a method is love."

~Martin Luther King Jr.

Foreword

This is not merely a must-read book, but one which should be passed down through generations to assure that the essence of Dr. King's message of social change, through nonviolent strategies, is correctly understood and appreciated.

As one who started in the civil rights movement, at Tennessee State University in 1960, I was privileged to witness firsthand and close up the impact of Dr. King's persona and the eloquence of his words as they challenged us as "the student foot soldiers of the movement."

When asked to reflect on this monumental work by Rev. Dr. Stephon Ferguson I was surprised, shocked and a little intimidated as to what I could share that would put in its proper perspective what the restating of the words of Dr. King would mean to this current generation. Were the words, articulated by Dr. Ferguson, going to be just another opportunity for someone to cash in on one of America's historical giants? I remembered when I first encountered Dr. Ferguson he was addressing, in Heritage Sanctuary of Ebenezer Baptist Church, a large group of tourists.

I sat quietly and listened as he articulated the often quoted "I Have a Dream" speech" it was profoundly different on that day than all of the other renditions that I had previously heard. I was there, in Washington, on August 28th and heard the original speech from the originator. However, as I sat in Ebenezer on that day and listened to this speaker, I knew that he instinctively was far more than an ordinary speech maker.

I researched his background to find out that he was an accomplished theological academician who had studied the life of Dr. King for more than two decades and had actually visited and spoken at many of the locations where Dr. King had spoken. He seemed to comprehend some of Dr. King's frustrations, pain, anxieties, disappointments, apprehensions and understood why he chose nonviolence as a strategy for social change.

I feel that Dr. Ferguson has a defined purpose to share not only the words of Dr. King, but to bring to life the source from whence Dr, King's philosophy of nonviolence was generated.

This book will, as it did for Dr. Ferguson and me, give you a purpose to pursue equity, justice, and freedom for all human beings. As you fully comprehended the subtle message of this book, your deep appreciation for what Dr. King did and continues to do for peace, throughout this divided nation, will be immeasurably enhanced.

Rev. Dr. Gerald L. Durley,
Pastor Emeritus - Providence Missionary Baptist Church -
Atlanta, Georgia
Dean Emeritus – Clark Atlanta University

Introduction

Born from the fight of our predecessors, I've long discovered that society today is comprised of diverse, evolving identities, beliefs, and values, which no individual has the power to completely suppress.

It's not from a lack of desire. History has already shown, in many cases, that there have been attempts to suppress this diversity—Mussolini, Hitler, and Stalin are those we know of, but unfortunately, this type of mindset exists everywhere. While individuals can have significant influence, no one person holds the power to entirely erase the deep-seated violence, hatred, or divisive forces that sometimes lead to conflict or war. Instead, we can begin to shift the tides through united, collective efforts.

Working diligently toward a more equitable and peaceful society is a responsibility. It's essential to celebrate progress, no matter how incremental, and maintain the momentum, pushing forward with hope and determination. Change, especially the meaningful and lasting kind, often comes step by step, challenge by challenge. The true tragedy lies not in slow progress but in inaction and the resignation of the status quo. It's not about achieving perfection overnight but making consistent, genuine efforts to better our world.

With the evolution of such negative mindsets, there will be forces opposing good and the type of unity that is inclusive and supportive of all. That has become human nature. As we take on the challenges that exist today, it's become imperative to reflect upon individual roles and our collective responsibilities in society. We all have them. The problem is that some refuse to contribute, yet they accept the benefits. Embedded within our shared history are the teachings and insights of leaders like Dr. Martin Luther King Jr., who won the Nobel Peace Prize and whose wisdom remains relevant today. Such leaders, having navigated the tumultuous waters of their times, offer us guidance, wisdom, and perspectives that transcend the confines of their eras.

Dr. King, in particular, fought social injustices and challenges that, in many ways, continue to echo in today's world. His emphasis on nonviolence, unity, love, and justice wasn't just a strategy for that period of time, the civil rights movement; he was a visionary, and it was a timeless philosophy for human beings to coexist—peacefully. He did not believe that violence would solve our problems, but instead, it would bring about negative results, and it has. His insights stemmed from deep introspection and a sharp observation of societal structures, making his teachings universally resonant. Therefore, while the contexts and challenges we face today might differ, the core wisdom of leaders like Dr. King has carved a path toward a more just and compassionate society. Their legacy, embedded in our shared history, reminds us of the ideals we must continually strive for and cannot abandon.

Dr. King was not solely a leader for the African American community; he was a leader for humanity, standing as a universal symbol of justice, equality, and peace, transcending the confines of racial categorization, guiding us toward a future where every individual is judged by their character rather than the color of their skin. While he played an instrumental role in advancing the rights of African Americans during the civil rights movement, his influence extended far beyond these borders. Dr. King's vision was one of inclusivity, where the shared values of humanity took precedence over divisive racial lines. His vision was panoramic, encapsulating the hopes of all marginalized and oppressed individuals. The need for this vision remains as relevant and resonant today as it was then.

Dr. King envisioned a society where the chains of prejudice, bigotry, and systemic inequities were broken. His proclamation of "...That one day..." was not just a dream but a clarion call, the voice of hope that created a path forward. What amplifies the significance of his words is their foundation in authenticity and conviction. His speeches weren't simply eloquent, enthusiastic outbursts of impassioned rhetoric. They reflected his deeply held beliefs, formed through personal experience and prolific understanding of the human spirit. Often, it's our darkest or worst moments that bring us to complete comprehension. Understanding isn't a sign of our perfection. It's a reflection of our compassion.

Dr. King didn't just talk about the dream. He lived it. Went to jail for it. Received death threats because of it. And he endured violence to catalyze change that cost him his life. The congruence between his words and actions and the consistent demonstration of his commitment to justice and equality makes his messages resonate powerfully—even today. Behind each utterance lay a thorough understanding of humanity's potential and a deep-seated belief in our collective ability to transform the world. The question is whether we believe that it is achievable today. If so, we must act upon that belief and commit to its pursuit. While challenges and naysayers will always be present, our collective striving toward a more inclusive and compassionate world signifies a hopeful trajectory.

Reviving his message is not just about paying homage; it's about recognizing the timeless nature of his teachings. Dr. King's words serve as a compass in a world that still struggles with division, hatred, misunderstanding, and violence. They remind us of the inherent worth of every individual, the strength in unity, and the transformative power of love and nonviolence. To truly honor his legacy, it's imperative that we remember his words and actively endeavor to bring his vision to fruition in our everyday actions and decisions. We must elevate them to the pinnacle of our existence.

Dr. King's methodology demonstrated that battles against deep-seated hatred and ignorance could be won without a single act of aggression and that change could be catalyzed with the formidable combination of resilience, determination, and a shared vision.

Today, as we navigate a world saturated with digital voices, the divergence of polarizing opinions, and a seemingly incessant cascade of global crises, it's all too simple to lose our sense of direction and faith. Often, our words, instead of being tools of unity, become weapons of division, setting the stage for conflict and, in turn, with it comes the erosion of our mental well-being. The simplicity of Dr. King's message of freedom, equality, justice, and love seems overshadowed by the complexities of our modern world. However, the true power of these values is best realized when practiced in challenging environments. When Rosa Parks made her courageous decision to keep her seat, it wasn't just an act of defiance; it became a catalyst for the civil rights movement. Her action illuminated Dr. King's belief in the power of nonviolent protests as a path to justice. This pivotal chapter in history isn't just a past victory for civil rights; it's a critical pathway for today, reminding us of the strides yet to be made. If we achieved so much then through peaceful resistance, imagine what we can accomplish now by embracing that same approach.

When we observe the problems of today, the hatred, violence, division—the isms—and the lack of faith, we must ask ourselves if we've done justice to Dr. King's dream. Some, yes, but enough, no. The progress achieved in civil rights, representation, and equality is commendable, yet the persisting undercurrents of prejudice, intolerance, division, and hate remind us that the journey is far from over.

To truly honor Dr. King's legacy, we must recognize that his mission was not exclusively about combating external forces of oppression but also confronting the biases, prejudices, and apathy within. Only by melding the power of our words with the purity of his principles can we steer our society toward a future where the dignity and worth of every individual are unequivocally acknowledged and celebrated.

The vision of a harmonious society that Dr. King passionately dreamt of isn't just a dream; it's a blueprint for a better tomorrow. Realizing his vision requires individual commitment and a collective effort. We owe it to the giants like Dr. King and the countless unsung heroes who marched alongside him to continue the journey. We owe it to ourselves to create a world where prejudice does not stifle our spirit. And most importantly, we owe it to future generations to leave a world where unity and love triumph over division and hate.

In essence, it's our responsibility to unite in purpose and ensure that every subsequent generation understands the enduring significance and potency of Dr. King's dream. Employing his teachings as our guide can pave the way for genuine and lasting progress.

Our history is rich with figures who, through their actions, unwavering beliefs, and sacrifices, have left indelible marks upon the collective consciousness of humanity. Their legacies serve as guidance, illuminating the pathways forward during times of uncertainty and doubt. To forget their contributions or to forgo the lessons they imparted is voluntarily surrendering the hard-won wisdom of past generations.

When an individual's actions and teachings have significantly influenced or transformed our lives, it's not merely a matter of respect but also one of prudence to study and understand their paths. Their methods, ideologies, and strategies can offer invaluable insights for replicating successes and circumventing potential pitfalls and societal discourse. Dr. King has left us in possession of a valuable blueprint. There's no need to start from scratch when proven pathways to success, particularly in humanitarian endeavors, have already been established. Dr. King's methods have been validated through their successes and are evident in the world we inhabit today. We are the living evidence of his influential outcomes.

Dr. King's endeavors aren't just historical anecdotes— they are living testaments of what unified purpose and determined action can achieve. Neglecting or overlooking such a legacy would be a severe oversight. Forgetting it would be nothing short of a tragic injustice. His work, based on principles of love, unity, and nonviolence, is universally applicable. If we teach future generations about Dr. King's legacy early, we can change the course of their mindset and their actions.

Some are already working to remove our history, and we must not allow it to happen, even if we hold ourselves responsible for teaching our children. Continuing on this path can address lingering issues of racial and social inequality and forge bonds of understanding and empathy in an increasingly divided world. While we work to understand many things, it's vital to grasp our authentic history, painful strides, and joyful accomplishments, for there may come a day when we're only presented with a narrative others want us to believe. Many who conveyed the truth are no longer with us or soon won't be— this is our responsibility.

Where personal narratives intertwine with pivotal moments and dynamic individuals, there often emerges a sense of purpose and direction. I've personally experienced this revelation. The parallels I've discovered between my life and Dr. King's—in ages, dates, or addresses—are beyond coincidences. They are gentle spiritual promptings, guiding me toward a deeper understanding of his convictions and the invaluable work he undertook. I aim to share a greater insight into his life from my eyes and how society can benefit from reigniting his teachings and vision as a means to an end to the hate and division plaguing us as a people and the rest of the world.

Your journey, though unique to you, is shaped by the overarching themes of destiny and purpose. Such serendipities are often more than mere coincidences; they are markers on the roadmap of your life, signaling that you are aligned with a higher calling. These moments encourage self-reflection, urging you to recognize the path you are destined to walk and the role you must play. In doing so, you'll not only be paying homage to the giants upon whose shoulders you stand but also providing shoulders for future generations to climb upon to better see the pathway forward.

As you endeavor to connect the past with the present, may you serve as the vital conduit, ensuring that the wisdom from our rich history is not lost. Instead, may it be harnessed to sculpt a more luminous and universally inclusive future.

39

S *tanding at the pulpit of the Dexter Avenue Baptist Church in Montgomery, Alabama, the same sacred space where Dr. Martin Luther King Jr. had once led* with grace and enthusiasm, his origin, I felt the gravity of history pressing upon me. Every inch of space seemed to reverberate with memories of struggles past, dreams vocalized, and a vision for a brighter, more equitable future. Its historical context magnified the day's significance and the alignment of numbers that once again seemed to underscore my path—it was April 4, 2007, marking thirty-nine years since the tragic day of Dr. King's assassination. And there I was, at the age of thirty-nine, at the nexus of personal, historical, and inconceivably vast significance.

The air was thick with anticipation. The quiet reverence settling over the congregation was palpable. Every soul present knew the connection between the past and the present. Each gaze directed at me asked a silent question, seeking assurance, guidance, and perhaps a spark of the same inspiration that had once filled this room. The pulpit before me wasn't just a platform; standing where Dr. King stood was an honor. The wooden beams, the pews, the stained-glass windows—all whispered tales of struggles, dreams, victories, and hope— echoed King.

With a deep breath, I felt a surge of responsibility, knowing that my voice would now resonate in a place where one of the most iconic voices of the 20th century once did. I *was not just speaking to the congregation before me, but to the legacy of Dr. King, to the countless souls who had marched and dreamt of a better future, and to the generations yet unborn.*

In this fleeting moment of introspection, I recognized the true power of destiny and how threads from our past can weave into our present, urging us forward in the pursuit of knowledge to carry forth a message of love, peace, and justice. The journey had only just begun.

I had embraced numerous speaking engagements, passionately reciting the words of Dr. King. While I felt a deep connection to his message and understood its significance, I discerned a deeper layer waiting to be uncovered. It would have been easy to take shortcuts and rely on what I thought I knew or heard, but I couldn't compromise authenticity. To preserve his true intentions, I aimed to convey Dr. King's message with unwavering accuracy.

Reciting Dr. King's words wasn't just a job; it was a sacred duty to educate new generations about his tireless work and enduring legacy. Why? Because the world sent us a grave reminder. Violence and hate were on the rise, casting ominous shadows over our society. Neither violence nor hate offered solutions to our problems.

Dr. King's deep understanding of nonviolence, rooted in his studies, became a personal experience shortly after he received his Ph.D. in Systematic Theology from Boston University in 1955. This transition from theory to practice coincided with the onset of the Montgomery Bus Boycott that winter. The Montgomery Bus Boycott of 1955 to 1956 was pivotal in the American civil rights movement. Sparked by Rosa Parks' refusal to give up her seat to a white passenger on a Montgomery, Alabama bus, the boycott represented a collective stand against racial segregation and discrimination, particularly in the public transportation system.

Dr. King, embracing Gandhian principles, chose to lead through example, eschewing bodyguards even in the face of constant threats to his life. The testing of his commitment to nonviolence came when, just a month into the boycott, the threat makers bombed his home. Dr. King's response, steeped in his faith and nonviolent philosophy, remained marked by love and forgiveness rather than retaliation.

For over a year, African Americans in Montgomery avoided using the buses, opting instead for carpooling, walking, or other forms of transportation. This peaceful protest, initiated by the Women's Political Council and led by Dr. Martin Luther King Jr., significantly impacted the city's transit system economically and drew national attention to the struggle for civil rights.

The boycott successfully concluded with a Supreme Court ruling that declared segregation on public buses unconstitutional, marking a significant victory in the fight against racial segregation and setting the stage for further civil rights advancements.

Through these experiences during the boycott, Dr. King witnessed and lived the transformative power of nonviolence. It became not just a strategy for the civil rights movement but a way of life applicable to all situations of conflict and injustice. He saw nonviolent resistance as the "guiding light" of the movement, a synthesis of Christ's spirit and motivation with Gandhi's method. This blend of spiritual depth and practical application became a linchpin of Dr. King's leadership and the broader struggle for civil rights.

After embarking on my journey to research and study Dr. King's life and principles until the time of this writing, I've witnessed a distressing surge in mass shootings, hate crimes, and division, primarily in recent years. Society is transforming into a world far from what Dr. King had envisioned we would get to—especially after all their progress. But we are not hopeless. The path to healing, I believed, lies in the understanding of Dr. King's principles of nonviolence. These principles held the key to a more just and harmonious world where his dream could become reality. The solution is to understand Dr. King's principles of nonviolence fully.

Assessing the impact of racism and division is a critical first step in facilitating meaningful change. This process thoroughly examines how these issues manifest in various sectors, including education, employment, healthcare, and law enforcement. It requires acknowledging systemic inequalities and understanding the historical context that has shaped current societal structures and those shaping them today.

Effecting change to heal the racial divide is a complex and ongoing endeavor. It does not suggest the complete eradication of racism but rather a commitment to continuous, concerted efforts aligned with Dr. Martin Luther King Jr.'s principles of nonviolence. These principles advocate for understanding, education, and dialogue to challenge injustice. They emphasize the importance of recognizing the humanity in everyone, fostering a sense of community, and rejecting retaliation with love and peaceful resistance.

Implementing these principles in today's context means promoting education and awareness about the roots and repercussions of racism and being diligent in nurturing a culture that values diversity and inclusion.

Our responsibility is that we must collectively be aware of facilitating open, honest conversations about race and discrimination, encouraging empathy, and understanding between different racial and ethnic groups.

If we want to encourage change, we must actively advocate for it. We can work toward reforms in institutions and legal frameworks to address racial disparities and promote equity.

As was implemented with the civil rights movement, mobilizing communities to take collective action against racism and supporting initiatives promoting racial harmony is effective with a peaceful strategy.

Today, the media is always watching, especially with social media and camera phones. Even if we think no one is watching, we must model nonviolent behavior and speak words to achieve the desired outcome. We show that we can achieve lasting change without violence by demonstrating peaceful means of protest and conflict resolution. We contribute to a healthier and stronger society through forgiveness, encouraging attitudes, and seeking to heal past wounds through reconciliation efforts.

By integrating these principles into societal structures and individual behaviors, we can work toward mitigating the effects of racism and division, which can lead to a closer transition, to a more equitable and cohesive society.

Chapter 1
A Child of God

Born in the year that Dr. Martin Luther King Jr. tragically left this world, my life is interwoven with the number thirty-nine. By a twist of destiny, I was thirty-nine days old when the world said goodbye to Dr. King on April 9. He was, poignantly, thirty-nine years old. My father, too, was thirty-nine at that time. And, almost as if the universe were penning a poetic ode, I came into this world at 3:09 p.m. This number mirrors the historic 309 S. Jackson Street address in Montgomery, Alabama, where Dr. King and Coretta Scott King took their initial steps in the civil rights movement.

These synchronicities weren't just numbers. They seemed to be a sign, perhaps urging me to recognize, reflect upon, and help continue sharing the legacy of the monumental work initiated at that address. Specific alignments resonate with depth beyond mere coincidence in the intricate twist of fate and history. Aware of these discerning connections with renewed clarity and an awakened sense of purpose, I couldn't help but attune my senses to the whispers of destiny. Each day became an exploration, a journey deeper into the recesses of my soul and the world around me. It seemed the universe unfolded a map before me, showing paths I hadn't noticed before. Guided by the thoughts and beliefs Dr. King championed and the divine call I felt so strongly,

I began to align my endeavors with this newfound vision.

The more I listened, the more precise the message became. Every interaction, every setback, and every success seemed to reiterate the same sentiment: to be an agent of change, to spread love and understanding, and to champion Dr. King's philosophies of justice and equality in a world still in need.

In embracing this path, I realized that destiny isn't a predetermined point on a map but a journey of understanding and evolving. As I continued to dig deeper, I unveiled my purpose and the contributions I could make to the world around me.

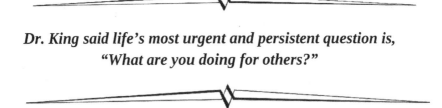

Dr. King said life's most urgent and persistent question is, "What are you doing for others?"

On graduation day from high school, the tassels on our graduation caps swayed with promise and potential. Two days later, my journey took flight as I boarded a plane to El Paso, Texas, after enlisting in the Army. College had never been a highlighted path in the scope of my vision. Its absence was neither due to my lack of ambition nor the dreams my parents held for me. With twelve of us, ten from my father's union with my mother, their resources were spread thin. Aware of my parents' inability to fund college, I envisioned the Army not just as a means of protecting our country or jumping out of airplanes, which my brother inspired me, Deonesus, but also as a gateway to education.

During the peak of summer 1986 —June, July, and August—I completed basic training in the scorching deserts of New Mexico. After graduation, I attended a twelve-week combat medic school program at Fort Sam Houston in San Antonio, Texas. My first assignment was at Carlisle Barracks in Pennsylvania, where I worked as a medic in a clinic. My subsequent posting was at Fort Meade, Maryland.

I spent less than a year at Fort Meade before a stateside swap took me to what was then known as Fort Bragg. In light of the 2020 George Floyd protests, the base underwent a name change from Fort Bragg to Fort Liberty, reflecting a move away from its Confederate-named legacy. There, I took on the role of line medic for a Field Artillery Unit. If anyone from the artillery battery fell ill or required medical assistance, I was one of the "go-to" medics. Although I was part of an airborne unit, I was not airborne-trained.

My unit sent me to Fort Benning, Georgia for a three- week jump school, where I earned my jump wings. To complete the course, we were required to make five jumps out of an aircraft, one of which had to be during the night. After successfully finishing school, I returned to Fort Liberty, still working as a line medic, but now with the added responsibility of jumping. It was customary for medics to jump first. We would position ourselves at the plane's doors, one on each side, ensuring we could touch down promptly and provide medical aid if any jumper sustained injuries during the descent.

Later, I returned to Fort Sam Houston for a three-month stint at the medical non-commissioned officer (NCO) school. A month after completing this training, I advanced to the rank E-5. Having my mom pin my rank on one side of my uniform was special.

My commander pinned it on the other. It was an accomplishment, considering I had started as an E-1 and climbed to Sergeant in only twenty months. By age twenty, I was a Sergeant, old enough to serve, lead, and risk my life for my country, yet I was still legally too young to purchase a beer.

During my final year at Fort Bragg, Fort Liberty, I became a Medical NCO at a Troop Medical Clinic. There, I dealt with outpatients, preparing them for their appointments with the doctor, akin to a nurse's role in the civilian sector. While I maintained my association with the same unit and continued participating in a few jumps every month, my total jump count reached twenty-seven from planes and one additional jump from a helicopter. Occasionally, I wouldn't jump with the unit to support the operation from the ground.

My active-duty service spanned four years, one month, and nine days. Following that, I spent three years in an inactive standby role, poised to be called upon if a war erupted. And there was a conflict. The Gulf War flared up in Iraq just two months after my active duty ended. Upon my departure from the military at Fort Bragg in 1990, my unit honored me with a thoughtfully crafted wooden statue of Iron Mike. Beautifully engraved on it was the name they called me: "Top Dawg."

While serving in the Army, I developed a passion for music. When my Army career ended, I enjoyed the tactile sensation of DJ tables and the rhythm of spinning records, but only on a limited basis. I rapped more than DJing. During the day, I was part of Fayetteville's radio scene. My first foray into broadcasting was in 1995 at Flava 107.7 WLRD, a 5000-watt urban radio station. As time progressed, a central radio station in the vicinity acquired us. This acquisition marked the turning of fate's wheel, leading me onto a path I hadn't foreseen.

Fast forward six years, in the aftermath of the 9/11 tragedy, I joined WFNC, a news talk radio station.

It was part of a five-station cluster in Fayetteville, though Cumulus Broadcasting is headquartered in Atlanta. My voice became ubiquitous, echoing through radios, but my face remained an enigma. This invisibility allowed me to transcend racial perceptions as listeners connected purely with my voice, free from preconceived biases.

As the dawn of the new millennium approached, I stood at a pivotal juncture in my life. At thirty-two years old, I had navigated many experiences. I'd worn the badge of honor as a Sergeant in the U.S. Army and found my voice connecting with audiences as a radio personality. The entrepreneur in me had birthed ventures, spanning a balloon shop, a beauty supply store, a quaint café, a mixed tape shop nestled in the bustling flea market, and the local news magazine I proudly called *The Vision*. While my entrepreneurial spirit blazed fiercely, a more profound quest for purpose simmered within. I was no longer seeking another business endeavor. Instead, I had embarked on a journey to uncover my purpose.

Since I was young, I always imitated people. In elementary school, I'd get the newspaper and read it to Mom like a reporter. I didn't study Dr. Martin Luther King Jr. until I was in my thirties, but I used to DJ parties with my friend, mixing in Dr. King's records that my parents had of him.

One day, I practiced mixing while imitating Dr. King's "I Have a Dream," and my friend 'Nu Wave' heard me. He came in, looking around the corner, asking, "Is that you?"

Nodding affirmatively, knowing it caught him off guard, my face lit up, and we laughed.

He said, "Man, you should do this!"

"Do what?"

"Impersonate King!"

James Marshall Jr. influenced me to get into music when we were in high school. He was an undisputed master in a particular dance style, popping and locking. People knew him for his exceptional skill and flair, and his nickname, 'Nu Wave,' perfectly captured his innovative and trendsetting approach on the dance floor. His unique idea of impersonating Dr. Martin Luther King Jr. resonated with me, and he has since supported my endeavors.

To truly capture the essence of Dr. Martin Luther King Jr.'s oratory style, I embarked on a meticulous preparatory journey before memorizing his iconic *"I Have a Dream"* speech. This initial phase was all about immersion. For two weeks, I dedicated myself to repeatedly listening to the speech. This relentless repetition wasn't just about hearing the words. It was an exercise in absorbing Dr. King's unique rhythm, the nuances of his diction, the deliberate pace of his delivery, and the resonant tone that made his speeches so powerful and enduring. This immersive listening was my foundation, setting the stage for the following memorization and emulation.

Aurelia Mclean, whom I affectionately call Ria, isn't just a longtime close friend; she's the vibrant force behind my journey into embodying Dr. Martin Luther King Jr.'s legacy. When I first tapped into my uncanny ability to echo Dr. King's voice, it sparked a more profound curiosity within me. I plunged headfirst into learning about this iconic minister and civil rights leader, with Ria as support.

Ria transformed my home into a living classroom. Imagine entering any room, be it the kitchen, bedroom, or bathroom, and being greeted by Dr. King's stirring words. She even equipped my car and provided me with an iPod, ensuring Dr. King's speeches were my constant companions, no matter where I was.

But Ria's support continued beyond immersive audio experiences. She meticulously compiled three boxes of index cards packed with pivotal dates, places, events, and facts about

Dr. King, all arranged in a chronological reference of knowledge. She also crafted a comprehensive notebook of invaluable information about Dr. King for me to absorb and take in the contents.

I immersed myself in these resources, listening intently over a hundred times, and then began the rigorous memorization process. I aimed to repeat Dr. King's words with fidelity, embedding them in my mind just as he articulated them.

We all have someone who champions us. Dr. King had a robust network of people, including his close advisors and personal attorney, who supported, encouraged, uplifted, and protected him. Whether we see them is on us, but we must see people. Ria's dedication has been instrumental in my journey. Her vibrant energy and steadfast support have been nothing short of a blessing, fueling my passion for reloading Dr. King's legacy through my voice—so the younger generations continue to hear it, drawn to his power and wisdom.

It wasn't until August 23, 2003, that I stood under the shadow of Dr. King at Martin Luther King Jr. Park, not just as a member of a community committee but as an embodiment of the legend himself. By then, I had begun impersonating Dr. King by memorizing the five-minute segment of his iconic "I Have a Dream" speech. Day after day, I practiced for hours, gradually mastering two minutes of the speech at a time. Within a week, I had it down! Most people had not heard the whole speech, and that was only a third of it. Eventually, I learned the speech, about seventeen minutes long, with two minutes of applause. While my initial intentions were humble, impersonating Dr. King was done only among friends. Unknown to me, the universe had bigger plans.

Whether I was ready, ministry was my destined vocation. The calling ran deep in my lineage, with my parents and several siblings serving as ministers. While I hesitated at the threshold, God used the guiding light of Dr. King to steer me toward the pulpit.

In Pursuit of Purpose

Deep within me, the ministry pulsed like a heartbeat. It was in my DNA, a legacy passed down through generations, an expectation my parents and everyone who knew me held; convinced of my destiny in the pulpit. And perhaps they were right. After all, I loved God with an unwavering devotion; my heart was eternally tied to the well-being of people. Helping others was the only path that truly resonated spiritually.

In many ways, my life has always revolved around people. It was the reason I chose the medical field in the military. I wanted to work with people. Even my humor, infused with an innate sense of wit, was a conduit to connect with others. Conversations were my canvas, and listening was my art form. Pursuing knowledge was not just a passion but a ravenous hunger that drove me forward. Entrepreneurship was also in my blood, a testament to my unyielding spirit.

Yet, as I journeyed through life, I believed I was waiting for a higher calling. I yearned for God to choose me, to wield me as an instrument for His divine purpose, whatever that might entail. I was committed to giving my all if it meant standing in the pulpit, delivering sermons of hope and faith, or uplifting people through any means necessary. I was His servant.

While my purpose remained uncertain, it inevitably drew me to a different calling that felt as natural as breathing. As I ventured deeper into the life and work of Dr. King, the complexities of that era, and the monumental achievements of our predecessors, an unquenchable thirst for understanding *gripped my soul. I needed to bridge the gap between the words we hear today and the pain that birthed them.*

History, when fully embraced, has the power to transform us. It opens the floodgates of knowledge, offering insights, answers to lingering questions, and a humbling perspective on the sacrifices made. With each revelation, I experienced personal growth transcending anything I had ever known. And so, I continued searching, propelled by an insatiable desire to uncover the deeper truths hidden within our shared history.

Chapter 2
Retracing the Journey of a King

In 2004, a year after my inaugural performance emulating Dr. King, I sent a CD of my "I Have a Dream" performance at Fayetteville State University to each King family member. I wanted them to know about my work with recreating the words of Dr. King. At the time, I was also publishing a small local newspaper, *The Vision*, in my hometown of Fayetteville, North Carolina. I sent a copy of the latest issue with a story about the groundbreaking of the local Martin Luther King Jr. Park. I sent one to Coretta Scott King, Yolanda, Martin Luther III, Dexter, and Bernice King. The first response was from Barbara Harrison, Director of External Affairs, Strategic Partnerships and Programs at the Martin Luther King Jr. Center. It was an email letting me know they had received the CD and thanked me for my work.

It went on to inform me that I did not have official permission to recite King's words, that all King's speeches and sermons are copyrighted, and I must get clearance before using them. Mistakenly, I thought it was public domain. I moved forward with getting the permission.

The following communication I received was from Yolanda King, the first-born child of Coretta Scott, and Martin Luther King Jr., who lived in California. Her letter has been an inspiration to me all these years. Yolanda thanked me for sending her the CD and paper. She was glad to hear that I was taking her father's work into the school system. "There can never be enough opportunities to expose our young people to my father's vision," she wrote.

Whenever I speak to young people about Dr. King, I always remember Yolanda's words of encouragement. I never met Yolanda in person, but I met her spiritually, and it has been and continues to be a blessing.

It took an entire year before Intellectual Properties Management, the sole licensor of the Estate of Martin Luther King Jr., responded. They told me it was the first time they had ever granted an individual a license to use Dr. King's words. Most people recite his speeches occasionally, typically around Martin Luther King Jr. Day and Black History Month. However, this had become my work—my life's mission. There was no season.

A source of inspiration became a transformation.

In December 2005, I received the Intellectual Property Management (IPM) license. Coretta Scott King passed the following month, January 2006, after I received, via facsimile, permission from the Estate of Martin Luther King Jr. to recite her husband's copyrighted speeches and sermons. Yolanda King died of heart failure on May 15, 2007, fifteen months after her mother. I never had the honor of meeting Yolanda or Mrs. King. Unfortunately, Dexter King passed away on January 22, 2024.

On the eve of Martin Luther King Jr.'s ninety-first birthday, January 14, 2020, Dr. Bernice King, CEO of The King Center, unveiled the new name of the center's theater in her sister's honor, The Yolanda D. King Theatre for Performing Arts.

Bernice told the Atlanta Journal-Constitution that Yolanda King founded The King Center's Cultural Affairs Department. She often used the theater to present and perform plays about social justice and equality for a nonviolent film festival.

During a Black History Month event at Fayetteville State University, I was honored to deliver a speech as Dr. King. Among the audience members was Senator Larry Shaw, who was deeply impressed by my portrayal and the uncanny resonance of Dr. King. His appreciation led to an invitation I will always cherish: the opportunity to present Dr. King's iconic "I Have a Dream" at the North Carolina General Assembly.

On March 1, 2007, a date doubly significant as it coincided with my thirty-ninth birthday, I stood within the grandeur of the General Assembly. Supported by my close friends Herbert Miller and Aurelia McLean, who were in the audience, I addressed a captivated assembly. Palpable anticipation charged the atmosphere.

However, after observing the effect of my initial performance on the audience, I felt a compelling need to examine Dr. King's ethos further. I followed with his poignant piece, "Love Your Enemies." The room responded with a standing ovation, a sea of applause, even with Beverly Perdue, who would ascend to the governorship the following year, rising to her feet. She later approached me with words I'll never forget, sharing that she had yet to hear the speech delivered with such authenticity and enthusiasm.

As Senator Larry Shaw and I stepped out of the legislative building, we were immediately met by a wave of individuals, their questions coming in rapid succession. Each inquiry opened the door to new prospects, and from that singular presentation, a ripple effect began.

The buzz about my portrayal of Dr. King grew louder with each passing moment. Yet, I recognized an imperative. At thirty-five years of age, Martin Luther King Jr. became the youngest recipient of the Nobel Peace Prize. Upon learning of his distinction, he pledged the entire prize sum of $54,123 to advance the civil rights movement. That was one reason I needed to study and do extensive research into the life and legacy of the man I represented. It wasn't just about replicating his voice but about embodying his ethos. Dr. King's life has influenced me as a child of God because my work and beliefs trace back to his life and work as a Christian—a man of God. When viewing his life through the lens of spirituality, I realized that his call for a better world wasn't just laws and policies—it was about transforming hearts, mirroring the Christian call for personal and societal redemption. Dr. King's commitment to justice, love, and equality wasn't just political or societal—it was deeply spiritual. Dr. King imbued his teachings and actions with Christ's principles: love for one's neighbor, the call for the oppressed to be free, and the pursuit of righteousness and justice. Dr. King's life as a child of God meant recognizing that his battle for civil rights was, at its core, a spiritual quest to align the world with the teachings and love of Christ.

Dr. Martin Luther King Jr.'s life has influenced my journey, primarily through the lens of faith. As a child of God, I see Dr. King not just as a civil rights icon but also as a reminder of Christian values and how we can make them work to unite people to work for a greater goal—racial justice. Every stride he took, every speech he delivered, was deeply rooted in his unwavering faith in God. This divine connection fortified him with the strength to face the harrowing challenges of racism, stand resilient amidst criticism—even from fellow African Americans—and manage and sustain the responsibilities of being a pastor, a civil rights champion, a husband, and a father. Dr. King did all this while confronting constant death threats targeted at both him and his family.

While Dr. King's eloquent words have left an indelible mark, his actions—aligning his words and deeds—resonated. He was a scholar, amassing knowledge at every turn, but his wisdom set him apart. Knowledge is the act of knowing, while wisdom is the discernment to apply that knowledge judiciously. Dr. King was a living testament to this distinction.

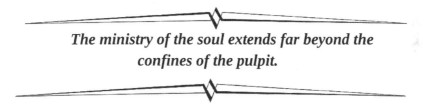

The ministry of the soul extends far beyond the confines of the pulpit.

The universal message of love was at the core of Dr. King's teachings. Jesus, when questioned about the paramount commandment, emphasized love—loving God wholeheartedly and loving one's neighbor as oneself. Dr. King mirrored this principle. In embracing genuine love for God and humanity, we inherently uphold all divine commandments, each infused with love's essence.

Today, we must try to revisit nonviolence. I was committed to honoring Dr. King's legacy to convey to the present and future the pressing significance of his beliefs, his ideology, and his dream because of his spiritual beliefs. It became paramount to explain why preserving Dr. King's dream was crucial and how we could ensure its realization by embracing and enacting his ideology and tenets.

Dr. Martin Luther King Jr.'s life and work offer a lens through which I understand the nuanced complexities of being Black—a minority. His journey elucidated the challenges of this identity and, more significantly, the tenacity and strategy required to navigate and surmount them.

Consider the young Martin, a six-year-old who abruptly discovered the realities of racial segregation when societal norms tore apart the bonds of a white childhood friendship. Or at fifteen, when he endured the humiliation, winning a speech contest for speaking about injustice and being told to relinquish his bus seat with his teacher and stand so a white passenger could occupy it. He stood in the bus aisle for the hours-long trip back to Atlanta after winning a regional oratorical contest where he spoke against such prejudices. These early experiences were but a precursor to his challenges later in life, including being a minority at the Crozer Theological Seminary. Yet, Dr. King emerged as the Valedictorian among his predominantly white peers. Dr. King knew from his experiences what being Black meant. From when he was six years old to his death, all I learned about Dr. King had an irrevocable impact on me. In addition, I better understood what being a minority meant and how to be in the majority as a minority strategically.

These pivotal moments in Dr. King's life have illuminated the art of turning adversity into advantage, illustrating that it's about learning to triumph against the stacked odds and bridge divides, even when it goes against popular sentiment. He demonstrated that we could choose to rise together in a sea of division.

For minorities, the path to success often requires heightened unity and strategy. As Malcolm X argued, "We're not outnumbered. We're outorganized." Dr. King's journey underscored that division is a long-employed tactic to maintain power imbalances. We see echoes of this in biblical times when the Pharaoh pitted enslaved Israelites against each other or in America during the Populist Movement. During that period, a significant development occurred as Black and White communities formed a growing alliance, posing a threat to the established power structure held by the Bourbon Interests. These Bourbon interests primarily represented business interests, showing general support for the objectives of the banking and railroad industries. However, they strongly opposed providing subsidies to these industries and were unwilling to shield them from competitive forces. The Bourbon Interests took legislative action in response to this emerging cooperation between Black and White communities. They enacted laws and regulations that effectively prohibited any form of collaboration between these racial groups. This legislative approach sowed the seeds of segregation in America, leading to the systemic racial divisions that persisted for years to come. This tactic of division is about more than just maintaining numerical superiority. It's about ensuring that policies and laws are crafted to perpetuate a status quo that benefits the oppressors at the expense of the oppressed.

Being a minority is more than just an identity marked by numerical difference. It encompasses our history, experiences, challenges, and triumphs. It means understanding the historical and societal dynamics and, more importantly, rallying together to pave the way for a more just and equitable society.

Dr. King influenced my perspective on leadership. Amid the tumultuous backdrop of the civil rights movement, numerous leaders and stalwarts emerged, championing justice and equality. Yet, Dr. King's indomitable spirit and unparalleled leadership acumen helped direct those roles and gifts. His approach was not just about confrontation but also about nurturing collaboration, unity, and a shared vision. Dr. King's ability to galvanize disparate energies into a focused movement has left an indelible mark on my leadership ethos.

To genuinely enlighten others about his monumental legacy, I needed to deeply engage in the crucibles and places that shaped his path. While reliving his experiences or fathoming the depths of his convictions was elusive, I strived to resonate as closely with them as possible. It was imperative to deeply connect with Dr. King's trials and dreams before vocalizing his words, ensuring that each utterance came from a place of sincere understanding and compassion. My journey was deliberate, a reminder that each of us must have a purpose to make a mark on the world.

Restoring Peace by Embracing Dr. King's Principles of Nonviolence

I had embraced numerous speaking engagements, passionately reciting the words of Dr. King. While I felt a deep connection to his message and understood its significance, I discerned a deeper layer waiting to be uncovered. It would have been easy to take shortcuts and rely on what I thought I knew or heard, but I couldn't compromise authenticity. To preserve his true intentions, I aimed to convey Dr. King's message with unwavering accuracy.

Reciting Dr. King's words wasn't just a job; it was a sacred duty to educate new generations about his tireless work and enduring legacy. Why? Because the world sent us a grave reminder. Violence and hate were on the rise, casting ominous shadows over our society. Neither violence nor hate offered solutions to our problems.

Dr. King's deep understanding of nonviolence, rooted in his studies, became a personal experience shortly after he received his Ph.D. in Systematic Theology from Boston University in 1955. This transition from theory to practice coincided with the onset of the Montgomery Bus Boycott that winter. The Montgomery Bus Boycott of 1955 to 1956 was pivotal in the American civil rights movement. Sparked by Rosa Parks' refusal to give up her seat to a white passenger on a Montgomery, Alabama bus, the boycott represented a collective stand against racial segregation and discrimination, particularly in the *public transportation system.*

Dr. King, embracing Gandhian principles, chose to lead through example, eschewing bodyguards even in the face of constant threats to his life. The testing of his commitment to nonviolence came when, just a month into the boycott, the threat makers bombed his home. Dr. King's response, steeped in his faith and nonviolent philosophy, remained marked by love and forgiveness rather than retaliation.

For over a year, African Americans in Montgomery avoided using the buses, opting instead for carpooling, walking, or other forms of transportation. This peaceful protest, led by Dr. Martin Luther King Jr., significantly impacted the city's transit system economically and drew national attention to the struggle for civil rights.

The boycott successfully concluded with a Supreme Court ruling that declared segregation on public buses unconstitutional, marking a significant victory in the fight against racial segregation and setting the stage for further civil rights advancements.

Through these experiences during the boycott, Dr. King witnessed and lived the transformative power of nonviolence. It became not just a strategy for the civil rights movement but a way of life applicable to all situations of conflict and injustice. He saw nonviolent resistance as the "guiding light" of the movement, a synthesis of Christ's spirit and motivation with Gandhi's method. This blend of spiritual depth and practical application became a linchpin of Dr. King's leadership and the broader struggle for civil rights.

After embarking on my journey to research and study Dr. King's life and principles until the time of this writing, I've witnessed a distressing surge in mass shootings, hate crimes, and division, primarily in recent years. Society is transforming into a world far from what Dr. King had envisioned we would get to—especially after all their progress. But we are not hopeless. The path to healing, I believed, lies in the understanding of Dr. King's principles of nonviolence. These principles held the key to a more just and harmonious world where his dream could become reality. The solution is to understand Dr. King's principles of nonviolence fully.

Assessing the impact of racism and division is a critical first step in facilitating meaningful change. This process thoroughly examines how these issues manifest in various sectors, including education, employment, healthcare, and law enforcement. It requires acknowledging systemic inequalities and understanding the historical context that has shaped current societal structures and those shaping them today.

Effecting change to heal the racial divide is a complex and ongoing endeavor. It does not suggest the complete eradication of racism but rather a commitment to continuous, concerted efforts aligned with Dr. Martin Luther King Jr.'s principles of nonviolence. These principles advocate for understanding, education, and dialogue to challenge injustice. They emphasize the importance of recognizing the humanity in everyone, fostering a sense of community, and rejecting retaliation with love and peaceful resistance.

Implementing these principles in today's context means promoting education and awareness about the roots and repercussions of racism and being diligent in nurturing a culture that values diversity and inclusion.

Our responsibility is that we must collectively be aware of facilitating open, honest conversations about race and discrimination, encouraging empathy and understanding between different racial and ethnic groups.

If we want to encourage change, we must actively advocate for it. We can work toward reforms in institutions and legal frameworks to address racial disparities and promote equity.

As was implemented with the civil rights movement, mobilizing communities to take collective action against racism and supporting initiatives promoting racial harmony is effective with a peaceful strategy.

Today, the media is always watching, especially with social media and camera phones. Even if we think no one is watching, we must model nonviolent behavior and speak words to achieve the desired outcome. We show that we can achieve lasting change without violence by demonstrating peaceful means of protest and conflict resolution. We contribute to a healthier and stronger society through forgiveness, encouraging attitudes, and seeking to heal past wounds through reconciliation efforts.

By integrating these principles into societal structures and individual behaviors, we can work toward mitigating the effects of racism and division, which can lead to a closer transition to a more equitable and cohesive society.

Chapter 3
Imprints of Time

On April 4, 2007, I embarked on an enlightening expedition with my good friend, Herbert Miller, to trace aspects of Dr. King's monumental path. Our rendezvous point was Raleigh, North Carolina's capital, approximately an hour's drive from my Fayetteville, North Carolina home. The bus tour began in Atlanta, Georgia, and ended in Memphis, Tennessee. We were to visit fourteen historic sites along the way.

The pain was discernible in the air when we stopped in Selma, and the quieting naturally occurred. I knew what happened in Selma was instrumental in pushing us forward, and I needed to learn that history. There, a large assembly of nearly 600 long-suffering civil rights marchers, led by Hosea Williams and John Lewis, had gathered peacefully across the Edmund Pettus Bridge to the capital of Montgomery to exercise African Americans' right to vote. We received a high- level overview but needed to take the fifty-four-mile march. Somehow, I felt called to march and was sure I'd return.

As we traveled to the next stop, my mind shook with fury and fear that we had not moved society away from this country's growing violence, hate crimes, and surmountable division. However, what became increasingly evident to me as we traversed these hallowed grounds was the existence of stories—deep, painful, resonating narratives—that no textbook could genuinely encapsulate. Only those who were there, who united and marched, who lived through the violence and atrocities and passed down such accurate accounts, know. The spirit of these sites conveyed lessons and emotions far beyond written words. Our collective introspection in Selma was so inspiring that it delayed our arrival in Montgomery.

Montgomery was a significant hub for Alabama's domestic slave trade and the Ku Klux Klan. Like several southern states, the trade spread across many locations. The city's riverfront and rail facilities provided convenient transit routes, and by the mid-19th century, Montgomery had become a significant center for slave traders and auctions. The Commerce Street and Dexter Avenue areas, in particular, were known sites where enslaved Africans were held, sold, and bought. I observed the trail markers, memorials, and institutions that address our painful chapter in history and its long-lasting implications.

When we arrived in Montgomery, we stopped in front of The Southern Poverty Law Center, a block from Dr. King's church, Dexter Avenue Baptist Church. While everyone fixated on the waterfall out front, with the forty names of courageous souls who lost their lives in the struggle for civil rights, I decided to stroll on down with my eyes on the steeple of Dr. King's church, Dexter Avenue Baptist Church, originally called the Second Colored Baptist Church, although it was closed to tours. The history alone was fascinating, and it was renamed Dexter Avenue in honor of the city's founder, then Dexter Avenue King Memorial Baptist Church, in memory of Dr. King. I'd never been there and wanted to ensure I at least went down to the only church where Dr. King ever served as Senior Pastor. Herbert stayed by the Poverty Law Center with everyone else.

When heading down the hill toward the church, recording on my camcorder, my lens caught the attention of a man slowly walking around the church, seemingly in thoughtful reflection.

When I was close enough, the gentleman stopped and asked, "Are you getting some good pictures?"

"Yes, Sir," I replied, shaking his hand.

"Are you having a good day?" he asked, smiling. "I am. Are you a member of the church?"

"Well, I'm Pastor Michael Thurman. Every day, I walk around the church and pray for the members and for God's work to be done," he began.

As Reverend Thurman spoke about the church and its rich history, I listened attentively, fully immersed in the wealth of information he imparted. Eventually, the conversation turned, and Reverend Thurman began posing questions to me. In response, I shared details about my work centered around Dr. King and followed up with a brief impersonation.

"Oh, man! You sound like him!" He exclaimed, releasing unbridled enthusiasm. Clasping his hands together, he suggested, "Why don't you come on in the church?" and headed toward it.

He opened the door and led me into the church's basement, which was on the ground level from the outside and where the tour of the church began.

On those walls, I saw murals with such emotional depth and radiant hues that they captured the essence of human emotion and artistic brilliance, bringing tears to my eyes. The artist and Dexter deacon John W. Feagin created the breathtaking 10 ft by 47 ft mural vividly chronicling Dr. King's journey from Montgomery to Memphis during the civil rights movement. The masterful work displayed the harsh realities of segregated facilities from the Jim Crow era. Beyond that, it poignantly illustrated the struggles, heartaches, prejudices, and pivotal figures that shaped the subsequent civil rights movement. The mural methodically charts the arduous path toward equality in America, which was significantly galvanized under Dr. King's inspirational leadership, starting with Rosa Parks—the bus boycott. It wasn't easy to move away from Dr. King, depicted as an angel ascending into heaven, as so many things were going on in my mind. The podium used at the end of the Selma to Montgomery March was in the basement. I stood inside the annals of Black history. Reverend Thurman called for his ministers, who were in other rooms. Approximately seven men came down into the basement and stood in front of me. It was silent for a moment; no one spoke.

Then, Reverend Thurman introduced me to the ministers and explained, "I met this young gentleman while doing my daily walk around the church." He glanced at me and instructed enthusiastically, "Give them some of what you gave me outside!"

Clearing my throat, I recited a short piece by Dr. King, and when I finished, Reverend Thurman, appearing even more delighted, asked me to go upstairs into the sanctuary, get in the pulpit, and do one of King's speeches.

In utter disbelief at what had transpired, I pulled out my phone and excitedly called Herbert, asking him to hurry to the church. He was shocked that I was inside since we missed our tour due to the delay in Selma. But he got there and recorded me.

Within those hallowed walls, the pews, whose rich history dates back to 1889, remained silent but evocative. These were the seats that once cradled Dr. King's congregation. Although unoccupied, the resonance of their stories remained, with a strong feeling of their presence.

Yet, the revelation of that moment was my unwavering acceptance of the momentous challenge—to stand within the sacred confines of Dr. King's pulpit. In that moment, I occupied the space where Dr. Martin Luther King Jr. had once stood, delivering his fiery sermons to a congregation hungry for justice and equality. And there, in that sacred pulpit, I had the privilege of reciting one of his iconic speeches, becoming a vessel for his enduring message. It was an act of deep reverence and humility, one that unfolded on the 39th anniversary of his tragic assassination, lending an even greater gravity to the occasion. At thirty-nine years old, I was the same age Dr. King lived to be when he delivered his speech from his church in Dexter, after which he and Coretta named their youngest son.

I knew this didn't happen by chance. It was divinely orchestrated. An epiphany dawned upon me. It became clear that God had envisioned a purpose for my journey, desiring to convey a message through me—one that resonated with love, peace, justice, and equality. The legacy of Dr. Martin Luther King Jr. emerged as my compass, illuminating the path to my authentic vocation. Rather than me seeking this purpose, it seemingly chose me.

At first, embodying Dr. King's persona felt overwhelming and uncertain. Yet, as I immersed myself in the depths of his words, a growing fascination took root. That drove my dedication to understanding his speeches, writings, and the essence of the man himself. I endeavored to grasp the true resonance of his words, the force behind his actions, and the transformative milestones of his life. The insights I garnered were nothing short of transformative.

In the subsequent year, I relocated to Atlanta, Georgia, just one block away from Dr. King's birthplace in the heart of downtown Atlanta. I resided in Congressional District 5, where John Lewis served in the House of Representatives. Given my involvement in various functions and events, I frequently crossed paths with John Lewis. I was honored to deliver a speech as Dr. King at his residence while in Atlanta. Meeting and observing John Lewis was an invaluable lesson in servitude and humility, causing me to probe further into our history.

"The path to healing, I believed, lies in the understanding of Dr. King's principles of nonviolence."

-from the Chapter Restoring Peace by Embracing Dr. King's Principles of Nonviolence

Introspection

Dr. King's teachings and philosophies can potentially address many of society's challenges. If we genuinely embraced his principles, we could make significant strides toward a culture rooted in nonviolence. It does not make us passive; it makes us Christians, those who believe in peace, equality, and intellectual ways of communication and resolving injustices, systemic hate, and racism.

A foundation built on love can mitigate hatred and division. Some may argue the solution is more complex, but love can pave the way for dialogue, understanding, compromise, and education. Many of today's societal struggles are deeply rooted in hatred, leading to division and weakening the societal fabric.

Racism, once covert, is now overtly manifesting. This increasing visibility exacerbates the already existing tensions. Racism is not getting worse. The digital age provides tools to shed light on it now, more than ever before. The incidents now captured and disseminated amplify existing anger and resentment. Disturbingly, instead of universal condemnation, many either applaud, rationalize, or resonate with these hate-filled actions and words. Despite efforts, society has not effectively countered racism.

The pressing question becomes: How can we effect genuine change and eliminate this deep-seated hate? The answer. It begins with introspection. The external world mirrors our internal challenges. While media highlights isolated events, such issues persist nationwide, even within our communities.

We're often faced with stark reminders of the inner violence we inflict upon our own. Actual change necessitates first addressing issues within our immediate spheres—starting right at our doorsteps. To make lasting societal changes, we should consider embracing Dr. King's philosophy on nonviolence as a foundational step.

In today's world, where societal challenges and conflicts often seem insurmountable, the philosophy of nonviolence championed by Dr. King offers a timeless and practical blueprint for change. His approach is something that's needed. It's grounded in moral authority, which sets a high ethical standard for movements and resonates universally, appealing to a broad range of supporters. That range has continued to evolve. Its inclusive character opens the door for participation from various groups, ensuring accessibility to all, irrespective of race, culture, gender, age, or background. This aspect of inclusivity is a primary factor in its universal appeal and effectiveness.

More importantly, nonviolence requires sustainable change by addressing the root causes of social issues rather than simply treating their symptoms, which we've seen. This deep, transformative approach helps create lasting solutions beyond temporary fixes. Nonviolent strategies ensure a safer environment to facilitate dialogue and reconciliation by avoiding escalating conflicts.

In this world—often divided by opposing views, nonviolence cultivates empathy and understanding, bridging gaps between conflicting parties. It's about healing and uniting communities, making it essential for long-term societal health in a world of deteriorating mental health. The global success of nonviolent movements showcases its versatility and effectiveness across various cultural and political landscapes.

Adopting nonviolence as a way of life leads to personal growth and societal transformation, cultivating qualities like compassion, tolerance, and resilience, which are crucial for nurturing a peaceful and resilient society. In essence, Dr. King's philosophy of nonviolence isn't just a strategy for social change but a guiding principle—a blueprint for building a more equitable, inclusive, and peaceful world.

"A foundation built on love can mitigate hatred and division."
-from the chapter Introspection

Chapter 4
In the Footprints of Heroes

My search to comprehend Dr. King's teachings became a transformative force, reshaping my worldview, essence, and soul. Through his enlightened lens, I began to perceive the world anew. As I studied his foundational principles, they became the anchor of my journey, guiding and grounding me in ways I'd never imagined. I felt an unwavering compulsion to advocate for his message, rooted in a solid belief in divine guidance. Dr. King's monumental legacy resonates, and while I endeavor to continue his mission, I remain aware of the vastness of the legacy before me.

Interactions with those who knew and collaborated with Dr. King enriched my journey. Their firsthand accounts, stories of shared moments, personal struggles, laughter, jokes, and insights have inspired my mission with a sense of authenticity and depth. Many prolific accounts and information about that era remain scarcely known and have yet to grace the pages of history. What I discovered transcended historical records and pages. Specific details eluded adequate description or explanation; others remained locked within their private suffering.

Drawn almost magnetically, I revisited the deeply evocative trail of the initial March with James Bevel, Hosea Williams, and John Lewis, which was traveled again with Dr. King during the

1965 protests from Selma to Montgomery numerous times. Each step, trail marker, and conversation clarified what I previously believed.

I first embarked on this particular fifty-four-mile journey through the heart of the civil rights movement in 2012. The Selma to Montgomery National Trail took us to Selma, Alabama, a place steeped in historical significance. Selma boasts the largest historic district in Alabama, witnessing pivotal events like Bloody Sunday and Turnaround Tuesday. Before delving into the history of this town, our tour began at the iconic Brown Chapel AME Church, the headquarters for the voting rights movement. From this hallowed ground, the historic March from Selma to Montgomery began on that fateful day, March 7, 1965. It was somber! Humbling. It is unexplainable. There's an ineffable power in our gathering. We, united in purpose, deeply understand why we are here. We're collectively commemorating a monumental moment in history—Bloody Sunday—and all the tireless efforts that preceded it. It's a legacy we cannot allow to fade into oblivion. *We can't.*

Modeled after the historic 1965 march, we embarked on a journey of ten miles each day, spanning over five days. This time, I tread the emblematic fifty-four-mile journey with Al Sharpton and his National Action Network (NAN), a path historically marred with the blood of demonstrators who braved lethal animosity from local authorities and white vigilantes. One of the foremost civil rights organizations in the United States is NAN, boasting a network of chapters that spans the entire nation. It was established in 1991 under the leadership of Reverend Al Sharpton, operating in alignment with the spirit and legacy of Dr. Martin Luther King Jr., championing the cause of civil rights and social justice. The late, honorable John Lewis was present during that and every successive visit to Selma.

Since I spoke as Dr. King more frequently, I took this first trip with Michele Williams-Gore, my manager. I needed to feel our history even more deeply than the last trip in 2007, so I was determined to make the fifty-four-mile march. Michele had spoken with the leader of the Bridge Crossing Jubilee about my work regarding Dr. King. Just before the march that Sunday morning, they had a rally in front of Brown Chapel AME where I delivered Dr. King's speech "How Long, Not Long," receiving tremendous support and affirming reactions.

That was Dr. King's speech on the steps of the Alabama state capital at the end of the march. At the beginning of the march, a few thousand people gathered in front of the church, including people who were part of the original march. Civil Rights Leader and Congressman John Lewis stood on the top step to my right, which I discovered only after watching the video.

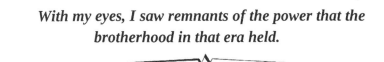

With my eyes, I saw remnants of the power that the brotherhood in that era held.

It was back in 2010 that I first met the esteemed John Lewis at Shaw University in Raleigh, North Carolina. He was among numerous other leaders of the civil rights movement gathered to commemorate the 50th Anniversary of SNCC, 1960. John Lewis held the distinguished role of president within the Student Nonviolent Coordinating Committee (SNCC) and was one of the prominent figures of the Big Six— Dr. Martin Luther King Jr. and Roy Wilkins from the NAACP, Whitney Young Jr. from the

National Urban League, James Farmer from the Congress of Racial Equality (CORE), and A. Philip Randolph from the Brotherhood of Sleeping Car Porters delivered speeches on the National Mall during the iconic March on Washington on August 28, 1963.

Meeting John Lewis left an impression, as he exemplified a rare humility. Once that event concluded, many other political leaders and notables rushed to make their way to the airport and return to their respective destinations. However, John Lewis remained behind. As he conversed with one individual in the parking lot, others gathered, forming an impromptu line to speak with him. It began with just a few feet of space, but soon, there was a queue of about ten people waiting their turn. One by one, John Lewis patiently listened to each person. In a matter of minutes, the line had grown to stretch the entire length of the parking lot; there were at least fifty individuals. Remarkably, John Lewis stood there for approximately two hours, greeting each person, ensuring he spoke to everyone who wished to engage with him. Witnessing this incredible display of his commitment left me in awe. At that point, I felt compelled to understand what drove this man, who had endured near-fatal encounters in his fight for justice. Courageous and dedicated are undoubtedly strong words, but they may not fully encapsulate the remarkable character of John Lewis. His unwavering commitment to justice, resilience in the face of adversity, and unyielding pursuit of civil rights make him a genuinely extraordinary historical figure with a resonating reverence.

Afterward, speaking on the church steps, a gentleman politely interrupted, stating, "Reverend Jesse Jackson would like to see you." He nodded in his direction and said, "He's right over there. In the front."

I spotted Reverend Jackson sporting a sharp black Fedora, but before I could introduce myself, he told me, "Man, you know they usually play a tape of King's speech! I thought they were playing a tape. And so, I'm hearing it and trying to see where it's coming from, and I look up there, and you're the tape!"

Reverend Jackson commended me for my work and for sounding "just like Dr. King." He invited me to his Rainbow Push Conference in Chicago three months later, where I spoke during the Ministerial Luncheon.

Retracing the Selma March and learning what they fought for could humble nearly anyone and dissolve hatred.

When the march commenced from the Brown Chapel AME, I immersed myself in the experience, absorbing every detail my mind could grasp. I wasn't alone. Determination radiated from the faces of every marcher as we followed in the hallowed footsteps of those who had blazed the trail, igniting change before us. The air, charged with our intense purpose and collective resolve, grew more assertive. Our unity was our greatest strength as we navigated the streets of Selma, Alabama, to the Edmund Pettus Bridge. We were not just a group of curious individuals but a formidable force bound by a common cause—raising awareness, the cause of justice, equality, and the importance of voting.

The expressions etched on our faces told the stories of countless individuals caught in the throes of history. We knew our road ahead was not riddled with hatred, brutality, or opposition. We were not marching to effect change but to understand the magnitude of the march further—to commemorate. I, too, reflected on the courage and unyielding determination it took to complete this march.

My thoughts turned to Jimmie Lee Jackson, Reverend James Reeb, Viola Liuzzo, and Jonathan Daniels—individuals who made the ultimate sacrifice. I pondered the raw strength that emanated from the legacy of those who had marched before us, paving the way for the justice and freedoms we enjoy today. It brought tears to my soul.

Each step I took revealed the determination of those pursuing the promise of a brighter, more equitable tomorrow— they echoed *King*. I let my imagination take me through that historic march.

When the marchers reached the Edmund Pettus Bridge, the streets were lined with over 150 state troopers. Over a megaphone, they heard, "I am Major John Cloud. This is an unlawful march. You have three minutes to disperse and return to your church," he said.

"Major, please give us a moment to kneel and pray," Hosea Williams asked, standing in unison with John Lewis, Amelia Boynton, James Bevel, and over 600 unarmed protesters.

In less than a minute and a half, the Major Cloud shouted, "Troopers advance!"

What was intended to be a dignified, peaceful protest evolved into a chilling display of unbridled hatred, with its victims locked inside the unsettling haze of tear gas. Brutal blows from Billy clubs and baseball bats fractured human skulls, and those on horseback didn't hesitate to use their whips with unrestrained ferocity. The crushing force of horse hooves bore down on fallen marchers while barbed wire-wrapped rubber tubes swung mercilessly at men, women, and children alike, young and old. Amelia Boynton and others nearly lost their lives. Until the day she passed away, Amelia Boynton fought for justice, mainly regarding voting. Disturbingly, many spectators not only cheered on the violence but actively joined in. Their hatred was allowed to be freely unleashed for everyone to see, and shotguns rang out, dispersing hatred in America.

Millions witnessed these horrors broadcast on their television screens, and demonstrations against the atrocities broke out across the country. Yet, the violence persisted without a sliver of consciousness for many others. If a child lost their life, this far-reaching brutal exhibition of racial hatred is somehow justified. This dark narrative has indelibly etched its place in history as Bloody Sunday. That was America, and we still have that same lack of consciousness today. There are Governor George Wallaces worldwide who will fight to the death to prevent progress. Through nonviolence, within our democracy, we can prove them wrong and effect meaningful change.

Two days later, on March 9, a significant moment known as Turnaround Tuesday unfolded. Despite the support of the Student Nonviolent Coordinating Committee (SNCC), James Bevel, and Hosea Williams, Dr. King found himself in a deep internal conflict about whether to proceed. It was a decision that he alone had to make.

His earlier appeal for a national call to action and a rally of hundreds of clergy members around the country had led to a diverse group of well over a thousand marchers committing to the arduous fifty-four-mile journey across the Edmund Pettus Bridge. However, their determined efforts were again met with a blockade of state troopers on Highway 80 and hate- filled concerned citizens. "This march will not continue. You can have your prayer and then return to your church," Major John Cloud shouted again through a megaphone.

Instead of confronting them, Dr. King halted the group and knelt in prayer, led by Reverend Ralph Abernathy—a move that would become eternally relevant. Unexpectedly, Major Cloud gave a command, and the troopers stepped aside.

Suspecting a trap set to breach a federal injunction against the march, Dr. King made the tactical decision to turn the marchers back to avoid another bloodbath. This choice drew criticism, with some branding him as a coward. Yet, Dr. King remained committed to our civil rights and persistent in his endeavors and strategic approach to change—a peaceful revolution.

On March 21, hatred ascended as police uncovered four homemade bombs in Black neighborhoods in Birmingham, Alabama. One was in a residence, another in a funeral home, a school, and a Black church. They were all diffused before the bombs went off. The march commenced for a third time from Brown Chapel AME Church in Selma with arms interlocked, an emblem of unity. I closed my eyes, imagining I was part of the peaceful protest with Dr. King at the helm and his wife, Coretta, by his side—to negotiate, demonstrate, and resist while raising white consciousness amid horrific displays of hatred. My ears heard the chorus beautifully singing what became the anthem of the civil rights movement, "We Shall Overcome."

Ignited with emotional turmoil, I took a deep breath, enveloping a greater understanding as we visited sites such as a Black farmer's field and areas along the side of the road where they would march approximately ten miles each day for five days and camp out. These cold and shivering fearless souls withstood freezing temperatures. Initially, the plan was to camp along the way, but due to the circumstances and snake sightings, Reverend

Sharpton and the team decided it would be safer not to camp by the roadside. Instead, we returned to the initial starting point, the church, and camped there. The following morning, after breakfast, the bus arrived and took us to the point where we had paused our journey the day before. As we continued the march, many fellow marchers, including some notable celebrities, converged in solidarity along the path toward our shared destination.

When our tour group approached the Edmund Pettus Bridge, I envisioned students, clergy members from across the country, diverse women, and children, young and old, marching in solidarity—a solid representation of what Dr. King believed this country could be. I felt it. My mind took rampant strides in conjuring more images on March 25, the collaborative efforts in St. Jude, where Dick Gregory, Nina Simone, Harry Belafonte, Sammy Davis Jr., Tony Bennett, Peter Paul, and Mary, and others joined the march among thousands who traveled across the country to witness the collaborative spirit of a movement that sought to redefine a nation.

The experience was humbling. One that left me overwhelmed with gratitude while my soul wept for the sacrifices they endured to secure the rights we now have. Even though it was a tour, this march made history feel vastly different.

Something I hadn't done until that point was acknowledge the intense frustrations that Dr. King, other civil rights leaders, and brave individuals of that era carried and lived with under the weight of their struggles. In the face of fear or with unwavering courage, they pressed onward together, driven by a steady commitment. Their dedication and resilience are an inspiration for us today.

Failing to grasp the significance of our voting history and the hard-fought right we exercise today amounts to a disservice to ourselves and the memory of those who marched and made the ultimate sacrifice for this fundamental right.

I drew a deep breath as my restless mind enveloped greater understanding. I continued visiting farmers' fields, where young and old camped in freezing temperatures. Along with historical markers explaining aspects of this history, it gave us harrowing details about the degree of hate marchers were up against and their experiences. It also told how the kindness of strangers offering support provided meals. Knowing our history, we must understand the relevance of what transpired and how we achieved substantial goals by having united. There is immense power and potential to bring meaningful change when collaborating and working harmoniously. The collective strength of individuals aligned toward a common goal can move mountains and overcome even the most daunting challenges. We can harness our shared determination and create a better world through unity.

Upon reflection, I understood that each generation may only remember if we return to our history. I needed to commit everything I learned and saw to memory. I memorized the entire *"Letter from Birmingham* Jail." It's about fifty minutes. Dr. King's letter from the Birmingham jail urges us to keep it in the community's consciousness. This history has already moved us forward, and we must protect and allow it to continue to do so.

During my educational venture into our history, I learned critical details that changed me. Some narratives and information may be outside the history books. Still, for everything we know, we cannot allow them to be forgotten or removed from schools, libraries, conversations, and teachings. We must protect it. I was sure I could only recite Dr. King's words with the depths of this history and understanding. I had to embrace them in every way possible, and this tour was only the beginning.

At the end of the march from Selma to Montgomery on March 25, 1965, a formidable crowd of more than 25,000 peaceful demonstrators converged at the Alabama State Capitol. However, Governor Wallace declined to engage with Dr. King. Undeterred, Dr. King delivered a historically uplifting speech, saying everyone asked, "How Long, Not Long," from the Capitol steps, rallying civil rights advocates to persist in their quest and never lose hope. He was right; the president signed the voting rights into law five months later.

In a poignant historical echo, Dr. King's protest on August 6, 1965, was the same chamber that witnessed President Abraham Lincoln inscribing the Emancipation Proclamation and became the birthplace of the Voting Rights Act. This monumental legislation outlawed literacy tests in twenty-six states, including the deeply contested grounds of Alabama. It shifted the power from local voter registrars to federal examiners—evidence of the shifting winds of justice. More importantly, it empowered the U.S. Attorney General to challenge and prosecute those state and local entities stubbornly clinging to an outdated and discriminatory poll tax. The act wasn't just a change in policy but a resonating declaration of our long-overdue rights.

Dr. King said, "We have not made a single gain in civil rights without determined legal and nonviolent pressure." This statement encapsulates the essence of the civil rights movement. We must engage in peaceful protest to bring attention to the issues, causes, policies, and laws and then address them by working to change laws from unjust to just.

"It may be true that the law cannot make a man love me, religion and education must do that. But the law can keep him from lynching me and I think that's pretty important too." King acknowledges that laws cannot force someone to have feelings of love or acceptance towards him. He suggests rather that the promotion of love and acceptance should come from the moral and ethical teachings that are undergirded with religious education and based on the universal ethic of love. At the same time, he recognizes the practical role of laws in preventing violence and protecting individuals from harm or discrimination. This quote is a profound reflection of King's belief in the importance of both moral teachings and legal protection in creating a just and equitable society.

We have the power. We have enough. We are enough. It is our responsibility to ensure that the rules are just. How? Who writes these laws? Our legislators. That's why voting and electing leaders who have our best interest in mind is one of the most significant nonviolent moves available. But we must go further.

There are three significant aspects of voting. Registering to vote, casting our ballot, and holding those we elect accountable. We can no longer be dissatisfied and complain. If the laws remain the same, there is no progress. The key is to change them together—United as one. Dr. King wasn't alone.

Still, today, we have a lot to fight for without violence. We must have the goal of participating in writing policies and enacting laws that reflect one nation under God, indivisible with liberty and justice for all. Many of these current policies and laws do not reflect the constitution that all men are created equal, and their creator endows them with certain inalienable rights stated in the Declaration of Independence, which include life, liberty, and the pursuit of happiness. Capping our progress in many areas, the list includes gerrymandering, systemic inequality, and lack of political power.

Our immense pain often drove the historical progress we endured. We rise when the burden becomes unbearable. The tragic stories of George Floyd, Breonna Taylor, and countless others illustrate that such pain is not isolated but shared by many. Unity and collective action often arise when our pain becomes a shared experience. It's a reminder that leaders closely tie their effectiveness to the commitment and solidarity of their followers. Pain can drive people to action, but we do not limit our responses to moments when the pain becomes unbearable.

Perhaps, today, those working to erase our history fear that if we follow Dr. King's blueprint, laid out in the history books, through intellectual conversations and educational opportunities such as this tour, we will rise globally, not just in America. The result? We will have empowered ourselves, which could create a peaceful and equal environment to live and successfully operate in. That is what is feared. We've got to be better aware of this intent and prevent the illuminated blueprint applicable to our success from being extinguished. We must engrave this history onto our hearts and each subsequent generation so we feel an innate responsibility to perpetuate its legacy through persistent action. We must continue to seek peaceful resolutions.

Marching once was a transformative experience, leaving me yearning for more. I was eager to continue learning, absorbing, and feeling the weight of the civil rights movement. The opportunity to march alongside revered figures like Reverend Jackson, John Lewis, and Dick Gregory from Selma to Montgomery was an unparalleled privilege.

This remarkable journey unfolded the following year as around fifty dedicated individuals embarked on a fifty-four-mile march. Our ranks swelled daily, with hundreds of others joining us, creating a powerful chorus advocating for justice and equality.

For we do not wrestle against flesh and blood, but against principalities, against powers, against the rulers of the darkness of this age, against spiritual hosts of wickedness in the heavenly places.
Ephesians 6:12 NKJV

The wrestle we face is not with individuals, but with the negative influences driving their actions. It's crucial to recognize that the core of our conflict lies with the harmful behaviors and tendencies that people may exhibit, not with their inherent nature. Remember, God created every person in God's image, *and* God is love. This divine origin suggests that each individual inherently possesses the capacity for love. External forces may have swayed them, but we must confront and overcome these forces, not the individuals themselves. Dr. King believed, "Hate cannot drive out hate: only love can do that. The beauty of nonviolence is that it seeks to break the chain reaction of evil."

Taking Charge of Change

*I*n today's world, we have collective responsibility. The demand for change resounds loudly, echoing through the persistent corridors of inequality. We have yet to escape or remove structural racism and the looming specters of race and gender bias that continue to cast long shadows over our collective aspirations. We yearn for political influence, improved healthcare, better job opportunities, and housing that meets our needs. Yet, all too often we find ourselves entangled in a web of inequality.

The power to enact transformation rests within our grasp, waiting for harnessing through unified efforts. The issue lies not in our capability but in our reluctance to seize the mantle of change ourselves. Often, we defer the responsibility to others, hoping they will shoulder the burden and right the wrongs. However, the truth is that we possess the agency to initiate change, even if it begins on a modest scale. Instead of idly standing by or remaining in a state of inertia, we can take proactive measures.

Collectively and consistently uniting to drive the change necessary for equality and justice empowers us and future generations. Through our unity, we thrive and stand firm and resolute in our peaceful pursuits, safeguarding equality, and nonviolence. Taking proactive action, instead of passively waiting for others to lead, is crucial in shaping a future where equality transcends from being a mere aspiration to becoming our lived reality. By initiating change, we demonstrate our commitment to the ideals we cherish. This active participation paves the way for a brighter future and reveals our collective strength.

Protecting our values in this journey is paramount. Our values act as a compass, and if you evaluate today's society, our values, or lack thereof, guide our actions and decisions. Chaos, hate, violence, greed, and division ensue because of this absence. Morals—upstanding values—are the foundation for a stable and prosperous society. When we safeguard these values of equality, justice, or freedom, we will align our efforts with the vision of the society we aspire to create. Upholding these principles is beneficial in cultivating an environment of lasting peace and prosperity. Through this dedication to our values, we can create a legacy of positive impact.

Chapter 5
Get Off My Shoulders

My endeavor wasn't merely a physical pilgrimage but a desire to connect more intimately with the weight of our history borne along this trail. Although embodying the spectrum of suffering and emotions experienced during those marches remains elusive, my soul yearned to resonate, even if faintly, with the deep-seated emotions that must have surged among those walking in solidarity with Dr. King.

During a visit to Jackson, Mississippi, I had the honor of conversing with the late Myrlie Evers, widow of civil rights icon Medgar Evers. Another poignant moment unfolded in Birmingham, Alabama, inside the solemn walls of the 16th Street Baptist Church, the heartrending site of a tragic bombing. I felt my soul swelling with pain. Amongst the descendants of the victims, I found myself channeling Dr. King, delivering the very eulogy he had once voiced within that hallowed hall. The expressions of those directly connected, who remembered, who felt the loss deeply, contrasted sharply with a broader society that often relegates this history to a single commemorative day, failing to grasp its prophetic relevance.

When I embarked on the journey of vocalizing and sharing Dr. King's speeches, as I took to the podium, I had yet to give a hollow presentation of his prolific words. I felt the obligation to embody the spirit behind them.

To appropriately enlighten others about his legacy, I fully immersed myself in the experiences and locations integral to his journey. Though it was impossible to grasp the severity and weight of his experiences or the magnitude and depths of his thoughts, I endeavored to come as close as humanly possible. It was paramount to deeply internalize Dr. King's struggles and aspirations before giving speeches and reciting his words from his experiences. I had to ensure every word I spoke resonated with genuine understanding and empathy. My journey was deliberate, a reminder that each of us must possess a purpose to make a mark on the world indeed.

The objective is not to repeat and recite; it is to effect change.

Annually, on the first Sunday of March, I find myself drawn to that iconic bridge, just as countless others have been for nearly sixty years. We each have our reasons, and mine is to continue to educate myself on the experiences of those who fought, marched, and lost their lives in the civil rights movement, ensuring that I never forget. Through this process, I empowered myself by having a more accurate narrative of what transpired, strengthening my ability to speak confidently and gain insights I can share with others. The annual march is a tribute to the brave individuals who sacrificed their lives for the fundamental right to vote. It also calls attention to the ongoing importance of exercising this right today. Many do not. I've been privileged to walk alongside luminaries such as John Lewis, Juanita Abernathy, Jesse Jackson, Al Sharpton, Harry Reid,

Cory Booker, MLK III, and numerous other influential figures in this commemoration.

Beneath the faded arches of the Edmund Pettus Bridge, the waters of the Alabama River received the ashes of Amelia Boynton Robinson in 2015. A centenarian at 104 and stalwart figure in the Selma civil rights movement, she had wished for this final resting place. Amelia Boynton was a victim of the brutality on Bloody Sunday. I was honored to speak at her memorial service.

The request to contribute to Miss Amelia Boynton's memorial service, echoing the words of Dr. King—a tribute to her indomitable spirit and legacy, moved me deeply. Miss Amelia Boynton was one of the most significant individuals in Selma. In 1990, Miss Boynton was awarded the Martin Luther King Jr. Freedom Medal for her contributions. I was grateful to have met Miss Boynton. The organizers tried to ensure that someone connected to the movement was at each stop.

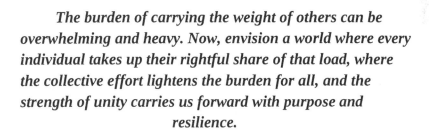

The burden of carrying the weight of others can be overwhelming and heavy. Now, envision a world where every individual takes up their rightful share of that load, where the collective effort lightens the burden for all, and the strength of unity carries us forward with purpose and resilience.

Her eyes narrowed to slits, blazed with intensity, while her face bore the immense weight of history—there were lines from the struggle, the fiery spirit of courage, the shadows of loss, and the myriad untold stories that had unfolded since 1911. Her rounded, aching shoulders spoke of fatigue as she firmly declared, "I am both elated and surprised to have lived this long, forty-seven years later. We often hear people say, 'We're standing on your shoulders.' But you know what? Please step off my shoulders. The foundation is only as strong as what you build upon it."

Locking eyes with this giant, my soul absorbed her words as a spoken truth by someone who, fully aware of the dangers, chose to march rather than merely observe or lament. She inserted herself into finding a solution, and she, too, knew what was needed. Miss Boynton had a pivotal role in shaping a more equitable society. Her presence at every stop on the tour was undeniable evidence of the struggles and sacrifices of her generation. When she spoke of the foundation her generation laid in 1965, she referred to the seminal moments of the civil rights era: the marches, protests, and other acts of civil disobedience that sought to dismantle systemic racism in America.

Martin Luther King Jr. warns, "The ultimate logic of racism is genocide."

Her assertion, "You're building on that," underscores her recognition that every subsequent generation is responsible for continuing the work, building on the gains made by those who came before. My generation. Your generation. The next generation, and the next. Should we forget and fail to keep our history at the forefront of our existence, what they have done will be for nothing, as we will cease to work together to create change.

Poignant and sharply denoting that we've taken history's work, sacrifices, and pain for granted, she warned us we must do our own. History itself has warned us! It was a call to action, challenging today's society to celebrate and continually applaud the past and those iconic figures who fought for justice and actively participated in shaping a brighter future. Miss Boynton signaled that revering and resting on the accomplishments of past generations isn't enough. It's not sufficient to merely stand on the shoulders of giants and bask in their achievements. Instead, every generation must engage, act, and build their history.

Today, with persistent racial, social, and economic disparities, her words are a call to action. It's an appeal for active engagement, emphasizing that while honoring the past is essential, it's equally crucial to recognize our current roles and responsibilities on a broader scale—a humanitarian one. Her reference to the building on the foundation highlights that it remains incomplete without the superstructure designed to support it, no matter how strong it is.

Education and awareness stand paramount in the journey toward a just and equitable society. We must dig into the annals of history and familiarize ourselves with the well- known and obscured narratives of civil rights movements and broader social justice endeavors. By immersing ourselves in these stories, we gain a more profound appreciation for the valuable sacrifices and develop an intricate understanding of each strategic battle.

If we are to make measurable progress, in which we will see societal changes, it requires broader community engagement. Our division is too wide, and we need to position ourselves to work together in totality. Still, we can achieve a more extensive collective effort if we align our thinking and goals. Nurturing environments for open dialogue and meaningful conversations is necessary. Whether through continued grassroots movements, enlightening community forums, or other local, statewide, and national engagements, these spaces offer insights into the pressing issues of our times and pave the way for crafting pertinent solutions that resonate with our community's and societal needs.

However, our efforts must extend beyond our community. Legislative activism is a linchpin in our pursuit of equity—it's part of Dr. King's blueprint. We must ardently advocate for comprehensive policies that directly challenge and address the roots of systemic inequities. We can instigate significant positive change by actively engaging with lawmakers, fulfilling our civic responsibilities like voting, and championing reforms—especially in pivotal areas like criminal justice, education, and housing.

At the same time, we still urgently need a cultural shift. Pervasive narratives perpetuating bias, prejudice, isms, and injustice in various mediums—from media to art and literature—must be rigorously challenged and redefined. By celebrating the rich fabric of diversity, championing the cause of inclusivity in every sphere, and consistently emphasizing the importance of empathy, we can sow the seeds for a transformative societal shift rather than stand on the shoulders of our predecessors.

We face significant and rapidly evolving challenges in today's world. Navigating this ever-evolving world requires continuous learning. That's our most potent tool. Challenges morph, situations change, and our adaptability becomes our strength as advocates for justice. We must stay attuned to the shifting landscapes of social justice struggles, always prepared to recalibrate our tactics, strategies, and focal points in response to the changing tides.

In encapsulating these thoughts, Miss Boynton's message

communicates that every generation's contributions are needed. It encapsulates the essence of our collective mission to revere and honor the storied past while remaining fiercely committed to actively sculpting a brighter, more equitable future. As she eloquently articulated, this imperative retains its urgency and relevance in today's world, urging us all to act with conviction and purpose. Her words were unscripted. They ascended from history—as a warning.

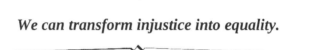

We can transform injustice into equality.

Comprehension of our identity and historical leaders contributes to carving paths to rectify the many issues we face. It's crucial for individual self-worth and collective progress. Recognizing who we are and confronting our challenges gives us a clearer sense of duty to our ancestors, families, society, and ourselves. It's essential to acknowledge that many of the issues we face today are deeply rooted in history and addressing them requires a comprehensive approach. Dr. King's legacy teaches us the power of collective action. History has shown that real change comes when people come together in large numbers and demand justice and equality. We've seen it work well with humanitarian efforts during natural disasters.

Dr. King's principles of nonviolent resistance remain relevant today. He understood that there are just and unjust laws and believed in civil disobedience to challenge inequitable laws and raise awareness about their injustice. He emphasized the moral responsibility to obey just laws and, conversely, the moral obligation to disobey unjust laws. Violence sadly marks our world, a never-ending cycle that begets more of the same. While violence might provide temporary relief, it inevitably resurfaces, perpetuating the cycle of hatred and suffering. It's time to consider an alternative approach, one that has proven effective in the past. His message is a powerful and transformative concept. It does not involve passive acceptance of wrongdoing but rather an unwavering commitment to love and compassion. This kind of love has the potential to disarm hatred and win over those who harbor it, or we will continue to feed hatred. The world is on display more than ever, and so is hate. We must stop it.

Context is critical when interpreting biblical teachings. When Jesus speaks of turning the other cheek, he emphasizes the importance of not allowing hate to dictate our responses. We demonstrate the transformative power of love by refusing to respond with hate when faced with hatred.

In today's world, characterized by division and conflict, love can change hearts and minds, leading to a more just and compassionate society. Even when it is happening, and we are breaking down or removing barriers of hate a little at a time, progress is still happening. Bridging the divide is a must. During this social and political turmoil, love and empathy can bridge divides, constructing understanding among people of different backgrounds, cultures, races, and beliefs.

Love encourages listening and open dialogue, essential for addressing systemic injustices and inequalities. With global challenges like the COVID pandemic, climate change, and racial tensions, love motivates individuals and communities to act with kindness and solidarity, prioritizing collective well-being over individual interests. Love and compassion encourage people to work together to save lives. This shift toward a more empathetic and inclusive mindset paves the way for policies and actions that reflect fairness, equity, and compassion, ultimately leading to a more united and equitable society.

Peace as Currency

W*hen there is no peace on a large scale, it's because there is no money in peace. Peace often remains elusive on a global or societal level because there isn't always a clear financial incentive to pursue it. In other words, when prioritizing economic interests or financial gains over promoting peace, conflicts, and tensions tend to persist.*

Consider the global arms trade, which is a multi-billion-dollar industry. Many countries and defense contractors profit immensely from manufacturing and selling weapons, often to regions plagued by conflicts. These arms sales can perpetuate violence and prolong disputes because there's a significant financial incentive for those involved in the arms trade to continue selling weapons.

This scenario may hinder peace efforts because various stakeholders are involved in continuing conflict. The economic gains derived from arms sales, which generate jobs and revenue, can sometimes take precedence over the pursuit of peace. As a result, international peace negotiations may struggle to progress, and conflicts may persist or escalate, often at the expense of human lives and stability, which we see today.

We must recognize the financial motivations that can obstruct peace initiatives. Achieving lasting peace sometimes requires a concerted effort to address the economic incentives perpetuating conflicts and find alternative ways to prioritize peacebuilding and conflict resolution. Today, our world is at the precipice of continuous, unsettling unrest. Our nation and the broader global community seem ensnared in persistent discord, with war erupting beyond our borders and within them— Ukraine, Israel, Gaza, the Central African Republic, Afghanistan, Syria, South Sudan, and others—are at war. The United States has internal battles—politics, discrimination, racism, sexism, and other ideologies, many of which stem from hate. Conflict is prevalent. There is no peace. Unfortunately, our default reactions have evolved into patterns of aggression and resentment. It's heart-wrenching to observe our propensity for conflict, even more so when the fallout of our battles harms the most vulnerable among us—especially our children, who often bear the brunt of our confrontations. However, they play no part in their creation.

The chasm of our ideological and cultural differences continues to deepen, obstructing mutual understanding and cooperative action. The looming specters of divisiveness and mistrust seemingly overshadow progress—compromise, diplomacy, and faith. In a world where the sound of war offers more tangible returns than the serenity of peace, we feel compelled to introspect: Beyond the economic implications, what are the moral, social, and existential costs we incur as we perpetuate this cycle of relentless conflict?

As we navigate this turbulent era, we must remember that our choices will shape our immediate future and leave an indelible mark on future generations. The work of Dr. King and past generations has left its mark on us. We can show our gratitude by reloading Dr. King's legacy and continuing to seek reconciliation, dialogue, and unity instead of being remembered as the generation prioritizing conflict over connection and discord over harmony. Embracing reconciliation means acknowledging and addressing past injustices, healing old wounds, and bridging existing divides. Engaging in open and honest dialogue is pivotal because it provides a platform for diverse perspectives to coalesce, nurturing mutual understanding and respect.

Unity isn't about suppressing differences but rallying around our shared goals and values to create a more cohesive society. By adopting these approaches, we're enriching our era and setting an exemplary path for future generations and this younger generation where violence is gaining momentum. We must show them that living in a peaceful and connected society can be an achievable aspiration despite challenges.

Chapter 6
Where Do We Go from Here

I n the wake of Amelia Boynton's legacy, as I reflected upon our departure, a resonant question echoed in my mind, perhaps mirroring the sentiments of many. What role do we, the inheritors of such a rich legacy, play in this current epoch? We find ourselves at a unique crossroads of history, armed with the wisdom of the past yet facing the uncertainties of the present. The mantle of responsibility weighs heavily upon our shoulders, urging us to think about how we might, as a united collective, shape the contours of our shared destiny.

Let me impress upon you the transformative power of education and understanding our intricate, hard-won history. Delving deep into our past reveals dates and events and resonant tales of perseverance, hope, and indomitable spirit. An undeniable change occurs once you immerse yourself in these stories and grasp the weight of the sacrifices made. It's as though every strand of your essence vibrates with a newfound purpose, compelling you to act. This knowledge will no longer just be informative; it becomes a driving force, shaping your perceptions, decisions, and actions in ways as it has me.

The narrative of our era is still unwritten, and its pages await the ink of our actions, choices, and resolve. The lessons from luminaries like Miss Boynton serve as both a guiding star and a challenge. It beckons us to rise, take the baton they've passed down, and continue the race with renewed vigor. While the struggles of generations past had their distinct challenges, our time presents its complexities, requiring ingenuity, unity, and a steadfast commitment to the ideals of justice, equity, and human dignity.

In essence, the question isn't just about our role but about our legacy. How will we be remembered? Look around. There's enough evidence indicating that we must be more than bystanders sitting around telling stories about the contributions of others than our own. As Miss Amelia Boynton emphasized, our role isn't to stand on the shoulders of those who fought for change. It's to be active architects in our lifetime. We must position ourselves to be a generation that took the foundational work of our predecessors and built upon it, amplifying their voices, sacrifices, and dreams and preparing the next generation by reminding and teaching them. If not, we are doing ourselves one of the biggest disservices of our lifetimes. I learned I didn't know half of what I thought I knew about our history. I could no longer allow the tides of complacency and indifference to erode the strides made.

The choice *is* ours, and the time *is* now. We can come together, draw strength from history and the boundless potential of our unity, to shape a future that not only honors the legacy of those like Amelia Boynton but also carves a path for future generations to continue, ensuring that their journey is one of hope, progress, and unyielding purpose.

In 1967, Dr. King and his wife, Coretta, took a trip to Jamaica for an entire month, where he completed the last book he wrote, *Where Do We Go from Here: Chaos or Community?* His analysis of American race relations and the movement following a decade of U.S. civil rights struggles was astute and multifaceted. He addressed nonviolent protest as a catalyst for change, American apartheid, the three evils, a shift to economic injustice, northern struggles, and increasing opposition. His book encapsulated his reflections on a broadly turbulent decade of civil rights activism, outlining the victories achieved and the challenges that awaited. His insistence on intertwining racial and economic justice was especially prescient and remains relevant today.

In light of our progress or lack of, that's the question that we must ask ourselves. Where do we go from here? Dr. King's poignant question is as relevant today as when he first posed it. Some may not have considered this question; they're comfortable with where they are. Yet, we have much more to do—to care about, change, and create; as substantial societal issues unfold, significant societal issues still threaten us. There is no peace. Dr. King's question prompts introspection, reflection, and a call to action that we must collectively work to address—to help heal the hearts, souls, and minds of society.

America was birthed on violence, and we have been violent ever since.
We must now question our contributions to this violence.

In the wake of the epoch-making strides in the civil rights era, it's vital to recognize the significant progress achieved. Yet, it's equally crucial to acknowledge where we've fallen short, where complacency has settled, or where systemic barriers persist.

Understanding our identity is a foundation of self-worth and responsibility. We owe it to our ancestors, families, and each other to grasp the issues, acknowledging that many persist across generations. Our current approaches to address these issues are insufficient, so why not examine what has succeeded in the past? What led the Supreme Court to declare segregation on public transportation unconstitutional? What compelled Congress to pass the Civil Rights Act and, the following year, the Voting Rights Act? The answer lies in collective action - people coming together to demand change. Consider the 50,000 individuals who boycotted city buses for 381 days or the quarter of a million who gathered at the National Mall six decades ago, including an estimated 50,000 white allies. This historic march from Selma to Montgomery, where thousands demanded voting rights for Black citizens, led to the swift passage of the Voting Rights Act just five months later.

It is crucial to recognize that segregation, separation, and division have historically been tools of the powerful to maintain their status while disempowering the poor, regardless of race. They still are. Education, particularly understanding the facts, empowers us to refute false narratives that drive wedges between us. It's time for a new Populist Movement 2.0, a love movement. This movement transcends partisan lines and unites people from diverse backgrounds to commit to justice, freedom, and equality—for all.

Our society stands at a crossroads like it did during Dr. King's era. We've seen the power of collective action, from grassroots movements to policy changes at the highest levels. The digital age and social media have amplified previously unheard voices, and the global community is more interconnected than ever. But with these advancements come new challenges: deepening political polarization, information manipulation, economic disparities, and ongoing racial and social injustices, all of which we've seen.

"Where do we go from here?" isn't rhetorical. It demands an answer from each of us, personally and collectively. It pushes us to reflect on our roles in shaping the future, our responsibilities, and our commitment to justice, equity, and inclusivity.

Whatever steps we take won't be uncomplicated or something universally agreed upon. Still, we can decide to seek an answer to that question. In that case, it will lead to effective dialogue, continuously educating ourselves, challenging our biases, and acting through voting, community involvement, or influencing change in our respective spheres. The path forward relies on our capacity to reimagine a world built on the principles Dr. King championed: love, nonviolence, justice, and community. As we grapple with contemporary challenges, let's remember his vision and strive to make it our shared reality. When I think I've learned enough, I haven't.

Taking a momentary pause in our fast-paced lives to reflect on the past is not just nostalgia; it's about grounding ourselves in history and understanding the foundation upon which we stand. Throughout time, countless individuals have made immense sacrifices, whether for the ideals of freedom, equality, justice, or the betterment of subsequent generations. These sacrifices range from the bloodshed in wars for independence to the peaceful protests and relentless advocacy of civil rights movements. I needed to continue feeling our history more intimately.

While we, the beneficiaries of these actions, may never fully grasp the depth of pain, the burning sting of tear gas, the bone-deep weariness from marches, or the heartache of seeing loved ones lost to the cause, we must make a constant, disciplined effort to honor those memories. Retracing our history isn't merely an academic endeavor but a journey of the soul, where we display gratitude, humility, and responsibility. It serves as a reminder that the liberties and privileges we enjoy today were not handed to us on a silver platter; they were fought for, often at significant personal cost, and their lives.

By immersing ourselves in our shared history, we pay tribute to those who paved the way and gain a deeper understanding of our role today. We must safeguard these hard-won freedoms and continue the fight wherever injustice remains. As the saying goes, those who do not learn history are doomed to repeat it. Understanding the past equips us to face today's challenges more adeptly, ensuring that the sacrifices were not in vain but beneficial to all future endeavors.

In reflecting upon the essence of a man, my thoughts gravitate first toward the family core—the sanctity of a spouse and the shared responsibility toward children. Dr. King embodies this paradigm, displaying his personal values and global vision. His relentless pursuit of knowledge sharpened his professional expertise and cemented his ethics, values, and integrity. Dr. King's devotion wasn't to collect individual accolades but to the collective upliftment of society, to manifest the dream of a beloved community. Even in the face of adversity, when standing up implied losing allies, facing ostracization, and even jeopardizing his existence, he didn't waver. He voiced his opposition to the Vietnam War, initiated by the same president who signed the Civil Rights Act and the Voting Rights Act. His assassination, precisely one year after his compelling speech in Riverside Church in New York on April 4, 1967, marks a tragic chapter in the legacy of a man who fearlessly spoke truth to power.

*All too frequently, we fail to truly listen. By not fully grasping the essence of a message,
we remain ill-equipped to devise effective solutions.*

Frequently, the media provides us with carefully curated clips, directing our attention toward specific aspects of a story. Nevertheless, it's essential to recognize that these clips may only partially convey the truth or capture the entire essence of the intended message. It's common to believe that we've gained a comprehensive understanding when we've heard what aligns with our preconceived notions. Yet, it's worth acknowledging that what resonates with us is only sometimes aligned with what we need to hear or learn. The information we receive can be selective, so we must seek a more comprehensive understanding beyond the surface.

Engaging in active listening is essential to truly grasp Dr. King's essence and the depth of his message. Instead of focusing solely on the often-quoted climax of his final speech, "I've Been to the Mountaintop," it's important to take the time to explore the entirety of his words and the broader context of his message. The genesis of Dr. King's forty-five-minute speech provides an intuitive understanding of his mindset. In a decisive moment of introspection, Dr. King envisages a conversation with God, where he's given the privilege of a panoramic overview of the history of humanity up to that point. He contemplates the Protestant Reformation's enthusiasm, the Emancipation Proclamation's landmark signing, and other monumental moments in this vast expanse of periods. But he says, of all the periods in history, he would want to live in the period in which he lived. That was his mountaintop, to see societal changes and people treated fairly and with dignity and respect. Dr. King explained, "But only when it is dark enough can you see the stars." He pulled the stars from the darkness and used them to light a path to freedom.

Dr. King's unwavering commitment to education propelled his professional growth, equipping him with the knowledge and eloquence to articulate his vision for change. His ethics and values, steeped in justice and equality, underscored his integrity, which is at the heart of all he pursued. His mission was to serve the greater good and realize the Beloved Community. Dr. King's courage was manifested in his willingness to confront injustice, even when it meant alienating friends, leaders, and access to influential circles, recognizing the potential peril it posed to his own life.

The teachings of Dr. King are still resonating with me, as they should each of us in some capacity.

I began to think critically about the direction of my life and—with the knowledge about Dr. King's life and the civil rights movement—where I go from here. I continued doing speaking engagements but speaking—as Dr. King and memorizing his words to recite—wasn't enough. I needed to understand their root and the carefully crafted words that influenced the mindset and behaviors of a nation.

On April 3, a day close to my heart as it marks the birthday of my only child and the day that Dr. King gave his last speech, "I've Been to the Mountaintop," I was privileged to perform for a distinguished organization that oversees aerospace in Atlanta. My journey to this opportunity began at the historic Ebenezer Baptist Church, where I had been giving presentations. Among the listeners was the chairman of this aerospace organization, who moved by my words, extended an invitation to address their group during Black History Month.

My speech resonated deeply with attendees affiliated with the airport, leading to yet another invitation. This collaboration with the King Center made the occasion even more poignant. Whenever I speak, I strive to channel Dr. King's spirit. I contemplate details, like the food he might have savored, the light-hearted jests he could have shared, and the counsel he might have given. But above all, I immersed myself in the challenges he faced during his time.

When invited to this particular event, I instinctively knew I would touch upon Dr. King's "I've Been to the Mountaintop" speech, commemorating its relevance to the occasion. Dr. King resigned from Dexter Avenue Baptist Church in Montgomery, the only church where he served as a pastor, marking a pivotal chapter in his life. Dr. King held the esteemed position of Senior Pastor at Dexter Avenue Baptist Church for six years, keeping it the sole church where he took on such a role. While Dr. King was the Co-Pastor of Ebenezer Baptist Church, he was alongside his father. However, Dexter stands unique in his journey, as it was there that Dr. King solely helmed the pastoral duties. In 1960, Dr. King made the significant move back to Atlanta, where he resumed his role as Co-Pastor at Ebenezer with his father, a position he held until his assassination.

One of Dr. King's motivations for relocating to Atlanta was its proximity to the city's airport. As his voice and message garnered attention nationwide, organizations and communities from coast to coast sought his presence. The convenience of being near a central travel hub like Atlanta's International Airport greatly facilitated his numerous speaking engagements. In 1957, three years before his return to Atlanta, Dr. King and his associates established the Southern Christian Leadership Conference (SCLC) in the city's heart.

I had the distinct honor of performing in a section of the airport close to the Chaplain's office. Present during my performance was Mrs. Barbara Harrison, who since 1983 has been the Senior Director. Enacting Dr. King's persona at the location he frequently traveled to and from, especially between 1960 and 1968, was deeply significant. It felt like a full-circle moment, retracing Dr. King's steps from his return to Atlanta until his tragic passing.

During the 50th Anniversary of Dr. King's assassination, I had the humbling opportunity to speak, echoing Dr. King's stirring words, "I've seen the Promised Land. I may not get there with you, but I want you to know tonight that we as a people will get to the Promised Land."

A Perspective Born from Knowledge

Throughout our lives, we are graced with the presence of specific individuals who not only guide and mentor us but also help illuminate the path we're destined to follow. *They instill belief in our dreams and stand as encouragement and support. Many such souls have enriched my life, and Mrs. Addie Richburg shines brightly among them. I didn't know her before she contacted me.*

It was after seeing a video of me speaking as Dr. King. She sent me an email and text. Mrs. Richburg introduced herself and shared their plans to commemorate the Martin Luther King Jr. holiday. She wanted me to be part of it. Mrs. Richburg said after hearing my voice and was blown away by how closely I resembled Dr. King. Then, she asked me my price. Generosity flowed from Mrs. Richburg's heart. She gave me more than I stated and encouraged me to continue my work. Mrs. Richburg knew people needed to hear Dr. King's speeches then and now. As time passed, she would invite me to be a speaker at an event she or the organization was hosting.

Change truly begins within, sparked by the unwavering belief in oneself. It's a powerful force, a guiding light that leads us through the journey of transformation—during the pursuit of knowledge. However, when this internal belief is echoed and reinforced by others, it takes on a new dimension. Their faith in us catalyzes our convictions, energizes our efforts, and shapes how the world perceives us and our aspirations. It's a symbiotic relationship where internal self- belief and external validation intertwine, creating a stronger, more resilient foundation for achieving our goals and realizing our dreams. That shared belief propels us forward and reshapes the narrative of our journey, allowing us to reach heights we might never have thought possible. Sometimes, we wonder if we are making a difference and if it truly matters. Yes, we are. And yes, it does. A spark from someone else can keep our passion illuminated, as well as the path ahead. Remember these people.

Mrs. Addie Richburg recognized that bringing Dr. King's voice to the forefront of this period could further inspire and enlighten many people. Embodying Dr. King's voice in these turbulent times has the power to inspire and ignite change. My work seamlessly aligned with the National Alliance of Faith and Justice mission, where Mrs. Richburg serves as president. She is also the Executive Director of the 400 Years of African American History Commission. God placed this woman in my life at the right time—during my MLK journey. She continually blessed me with wise words of inspiration and encouragement, further fueling my passion. Mrs. Richburg is a remarkable woman with excellent knowledge and commitment to service, faith, and justice. I am fortunate that God has allowed me to know this person.

When we embark on a quest for answers, especially when delving into history, as I have done, defining our objectives is necessary. Knowing what we're seeking helps us pinpoint where to direct our efforts. With its rich historical backdrop, Atlanta was ideal for me to reside. Often, we crave concise, straightforward answers, but the stories beneath the surface, the emotions behind the narratives, and the words themselves offer true clarity. I believed I would grow in my search in Atlanta the most, so I packed up and moved forward. I would find perspectives regarding Dr. King that would be born from unearthed knowledge.

There's no substitute for the depth of understanding we gain when actively seeking knowledge. If we rely solely on what others tell us, and they omit crucial information or get things wrong, we build our understanding on shaky ground. We mustn't shy away from pursuing truth, whether through studying the Bible, exploring history, or delving into our heritage. All these avenues give us a more comprehensive grasp of our identity and why we can affect change in our lives and society.

Throughout history, wars have been fought, lives lost, and hatred perpetuated without a complete understanding of the underlying reasons. Often, it's because individuals are born into a certain mindset or taught a particular belief system. That underscores the importance of caring about the origins of our mindset and beliefs. When we invest time in research and self-education, we provide an invaluable resource. Education holds immense worth, and knowledge wields substantial power—so much so that it can be perceived as a threat.

In our current environment, some forces strive to ensure we remain ignorant of our history, recognizing that this knowledge would empower us in ways others fear. Our race has endured hardships beyond the comprehension of many. However, through resilience and growth, successive generations have overcome these challenges.

Opportunities for growth and learning abound, and we should embrace them willingly. Sometimes, taking a step backward can ultimately propel us two steps forward. Seeking clarity and understanding offers a pathway to progress and equips us with the truth, which empowers us in our daily lives, entrepreneurial pursuits, and interactions with the world. It's crucial not to fear looking at life from different perspectives and through a clear, unbiased lens.

The mantle of responsibility weighs heavily upon our shoulders, urging us to think about how we might, as a united collective, shape the contours of our shared destiny.

-from chapter 6 Where Do We Go from Here

(Top to Bottom, L to R) Atlanta International Airport, Rev. Jesse Jackson- Brown Chapel AME, Rev. CT Vivian- Marriott Marquis Atlanta, Teatro Lope de Vega – Madrid Spain, John Maxwell Leadership Orlando World Center Marriott

(Top to Bottom, L to R) Historic Ebenezer Baptist Church entrance, Baltimore Maryland City Hall Rotunda, Brown Chapel AME Church Pulpit, Ebenezer Baptist Church Horizon Sanctuary, MLK International Chapel at Morehouse College.

(Top to Bottom) Martin Luther King Jr. National Historical Park Visitors Center, Sergeants Major Academy in El Paso, Texas, Steps of Brown Chapel AME Church where the March from Selma to Montgomery began.

(Top to Bottom, L to R) Ebenezer Baptist Church Heritage Sanctuary, Dr. Christine King Farris- sister of MLK, Rev. Dr. Joseph Lowery, Dr. Clayborne Carson, Speaking outside Heritage and Horizon Ebenezer Baptist Churches

(Top to Bottom, L to R) Ambassador Andrew Young, U.S. Army 20 years old, Presidential Volunteer Service Award from President Barack Obama, Article in the Fayetteville Observer, Great memories with the Late Great Dick Gregory.

(Top to Bottom, L to R) Marching with John Lewis- Senator Harry Reid, My good friend and close MLK friend Rev. Dr. Paul Brinson, Steps of Alabama State Capital – Montgomery, Alabama, Rev. Dr. Otis Moss, Jr. at Morehouse College

(Top to Bottom, L to R) **As seen in TIME Magazine March 02, 2020 for portraying MLK in *The March*, Edith Lee Payne- the face of the March on Washington- autograph and pose, First time meeting the Rev. Jesse Jackson**

(Top to Bottom, L to R) **With Congresswoman Sheila Jackson Lee- Senator Hillary Clinton- and Rev. Dr. Willam J. Barber II, U.S. Vice President Kamala Harris in Charleston SC, Singer Songwriter Musician Joan Baez, Attorney Fred Gray**

(Top to Bottom, L to R) Dexter Scott King, Dr. Bernard Lafayette, Cover of Atlanta Magazine's Connector Section, Isaac Newton Farris Jr. and MLKIII, Clarence B. Jones, Xernona Clayton, Ambassador Suzan Johnson Cook

(Top to Bottom, L to R) Marching with Rev. Jesse Jackson- Joe Biden- Al Sharpton- John Lewis – MLKIII- Juanita Abernathy, Memorial for SCLC President Rev. Howard Creecy, Jr., MLK Site Atlanta, March-Selma to Montgomery 2012

(Top to Bottom, L to R) From Memorial Service for Amelia Boynton Robinson, Minnijean Brown-Trickey of Little Rock 9, Naomi King , Article in Baltimore Sun, Manager Hilda Willis on set for *The March,* Georgia State Capitol.

(Top to Bottom, L to R) MLK NHP Visitors Center, Elisabeth and Afemo Omilami, First Meeting Dr. Bernice King, Dean Lawrence Carter, Ebenezer Baptist Church, Clarence B. Jones / Willie Ricks, William E. Flippin Sr., Les Brown

Chapter 7
An Ordinary Man's Extraordinary Faith

I n the summer of 1966, Dr. King took an audacious journey, leasing an apartment in Chicago's West Side slums to live among African Americans, the poor, and victims of injustice struggling with unjust housing practices. He became a resident, not just an advocate. That marked another pivotal moment in the civil rights movement, as the Chicago Freedom Movement signaled the bold expansion of their campaign, shifting the battleground from the familiar terrain of the South to the challenging urban landscapes of northern cities.

By this point in time, 2011, my travels had taken me far and wide, spreading Dr. King's powerful messages of nonviolence, love, and peace. I'd spoken twice at the Georgia State Capitol Rotunda for Coretta Scott King's birthday celebration, the North Carolina General Assembly, Stanford University, the Georgia Association of Black Elected Officials, the NAACP on multiple occasions (one where Kamala Harris was the keynote), and several conventions and events. However, when I decided to relocate to Atlanta, immersing myself in an environment rich with historical significance and the pages of Dr. King's legacy, I discovered the clarity of my purpose.

The Shotgun Houses are iconic duplexes that glimpse the living conditions of Atlanta's blue-collar workers during the early 1900s. Initially constructed by the Empire Textile Company to house its white mill workers, these homes saw a significant demographic shift following the 1906 Atlanta Race Massacre. As a result, African Americans began renting and residing in these houses, marking a transformation in the neighborhood's racial composition and history, by which I was surrounded.

The term "shotgun house" is believed to have originated from their distinctive linear architectural design. These houses were named this because a bullet fired through the front door could theoretically exit through the back door without hitting any obstructions. Another theory suggests the word "shotgun" may have its roots in the Yoruba language, specifically from the word "togun," which means "house" or "gathering place." This term reflects the historical and cultural influences on naming these unique homes.

When I moved to Atlanta in May 2011, I rented a loft two blocks from the King Center. In 2016, I lived at 484 Auburn Ave in one of the historic shotgun houses in the NPS. The homes displayed the socioeconomic diversity of residents in Dr. King's neighborhood during that period. From my front porch, I could glance to my left and see where Dr. King came into this world. To my right lay the eternal resting place of Dr. Martin Luther King Jr. and Coretta Scott King.

Many people who toured the historical park mistakenly believed my house was uninhabited, likely due to the sign that read "Private Residence." However, living there, I sat on my porch many mornings, writing, and listening to the resonant words of Dr. King emanating from a speaker diagonally across Boulevard. One morning, the lyrical cadence of Dr. King's voice resonated again through the airwaves, delivering his iconic speech that marked the culmination of the historic March from Selma to Montgomery in March 1965. Aptly titled "How Long, Not Long," this profoundly moving oration stirred the depths of my soul, evoking a more conscious awakening within me. I stood reflecting on the era of Martin Luther King Jr., as did those with curiosity and interest in learning more about him.

Driveways were a rarity in the neighborhood, particularly among the shotgun homes. Street parking is the norm; hundreds of pedestrians and tourists pass by daily. My prior five-year association with the park service had adequately prepared me for the bustling nature of the community before I made it to my home. My neighbor and I could easily open our windows and practically shake hands or pass an item between the tightly packed houses.

Relocating to Atlanta held a particular purpose for me— it brought me closer to the birthplace and core of Dr. Martin Luther King Jr.'s life and legacy. However, my involvement was minimal despite my proximity to the King Center. If not for the MLK National Historic Site, I might never have had the opportunity to perform or educate visitors about Dr. King's life and teachings.

Although revered by many, Dr. King was, at his core, an ordinary human being with flaws and imperfections, just like anyone else. However, what set him apart was his extraordinary response to an assignment he believed was given to him by God. People often placed him on a pedestal. Sometimes, when we look at individuals from such elevated positions, we may think we could never achieve what they did. However, Dr. King's greatness lay in his ability to address eternal life issues in a way that transcended the comprehension of some. He had a remarkable talent for effective communication and connecting emotionally and logically with people on their level.

What's not commonly known is that Dr. King had a strong sense of humor. He rarely showed that facet of his personality in public. But he was funny. Only his family and inner circle saw that side of him. People typically see him as the civil rights leader, father, husband, and preacher, but not the everyday man he was. One of his closest associates, Andrew Young, talks about how they had a pillow fight moments before his assassination. Dr. King ended a speech talking about the death threats he faced, and less than twenty-four hours later, someone assassinated Dr. King. Dr. King revealed a different side of himself in these intimate moments that the public rarely saw.

I gained invaluable insights into Dr. King's leadership skills and his work through my interactions with individuals who were part of his inner circle. Leaders like John Lewis, Andrew Young, Reverend C.T. Vivian, and Bernard Lafayette played a pivotal role in shaping my understanding. While people often say success depends on what you know or who you know, it's more about who knows you. I was truly fortunate to build meaningful relationships with many of these great leaders, to the extent they knew me personally, what I was seeking, and why. In their presence, I was like a sponge, eagerly absorbing all the wisdom of our history they willingly shared. The individuals who made remarkable contributions to our history want us to acknowledge their efforts and continue their legacy by continuing to make similar contributions.

I enjoyed getting to know Dr. King's close friend in Atlanta, Dr. Albert Paul Brinson. The two spent a lot of time together in Atlanta. Dr. King and his father, Daddy King ordained Dr. Brinson. He remains an active member of Ebenezer Baptist Church, maintaining a close connection with the King family.

Additionally, I had the honor of briefly conversing with Dr. King's sister on a few occasions.

I had the opportunity to travel to London, England, with Dr. King's only sister-in-law, Naomi King. While riding through LaGuardia and Heathrow on carts, I'd sit next to Naomi, who shared captivating stories about her husband, A.D., and his brother, M.L. King. That is the process of learning. To utterly understand and learn from those who have had access to or played a role in shaping our history, we must actively listen and pose questions that delve beneath the surface-level dialogue. It was an incredible experience. I even had the privilege of recording the audio for her book, *A.D. and M.L. King: Two Brothers Who Dared to Dream.*

Although I never met Coretta in person, I read her book, *My Life with Martin,* and listened to her tapes, conducting thorough research on her life. When Martin and Coretta first met, she was already deeply involved in social issues; she was more actively involved in politics than Dr. King. Her journey into activism began during her time at Antioch College in Ohio. Coretta became involved in the NAACP and other race-based organizations and continued her work for over four decades. She traveled across the globe, advocating for racial and economic justice, the rights of women and children, the dignity of the LGBTQ+ community, religious freedom, the welfare of the impoverished and homeless, full employment, and the pursuit of nuclear disarmament.

In my pursuit to understand Dr. King, I read Daddy King's autobiography. I was determined to comprehend Dr. King through those who worked alongside him and his family—his brother, sister, father, and wife. Those are people who know his most intimate aspects that weren't common knowledge. This comprehensive approach allowed me to appreciate Dr. King's leadership skills, cultivated from a young age, and the influence of significant individuals along his journey. His leadership philosophy of "Iron Sharpens Iron" left a lasting impression on me. It all begins with a foundation, often where the most profound truths lie.

"Darkness cannot drive out darkness; only light can do that."
Dr. Martin Luther King Jr.

As a Black man, one of the many lessons I've learned from Dr. King is the importance of self-care. He exemplified how taking care of yourself mentally, physically, and emotionally is vital for personal well-being and your ability to contribute positively to your family and the greater good. The era Dr. King lived through marked immense stress, hatred, pain, and loss, which continues to affect our community today. President Lyndon B. Johnson faced stress over the Vietnam War and the march for our rights. He was a manic-depressive President running the country. Stress can affect anyone of any race, in any position, at any time. What matters is recognizing the importance of our support system and proactively taking the essential steps to safeguard our mental health. Ignoring the significance of therapy or the effects of trauma is not an option. We must nurture the inner drive that fuels our resilience and well-being to keep moving forward. We can view asking for help as a weakness when it's a strength. Our brain health is critical.

Mental health remains a topic often shrouded in silence, and it's essential to remember that it's not always visible to the naked eye. Someone we know is struggling. Someone close to you is carrying more than they can manage, whether trauma, grief, or something else. They're students, parents, athletes, and diverse individuals. Globally, mental health is a concern we have not tackled, but we have options, and help is more readily available. The inadequate discourse surrounding mental health often forces individuals to battle their struggles in solitude. However, we can transform this narrative and encourage open, supportive conversations that promote healing and understanding.

Despite persistent adversity, Dr. King's commitment to nonviolence is a powerful demonstration of his accomplishments. He persisted despite overwhelming opposition, stress, death threats, and extortion by the FBI and continued to believe in the potential for change through unity. His belief, "You cannot solve a problem with anger or hatred. It takes empathy, patience, and compassion to overcome anger, hatred, and resentment," is something I've practiced and embraced. We must take more significant steps to avoid anger and hatred. There are healthy ways to calm our minds and manage our emotions in a society that aims to disrupt it with news, politics, corporate America, social media, and personal situations. The inability to cope has become more prevalent. We can't shrink and be afraid of letting people know when we're in these moments before we settle into them, and it gets worse. Talk to someone close to you, a pastor or therapist, but don't keep it inside. Do it when you need to step away from stressful situations to recalibrate.

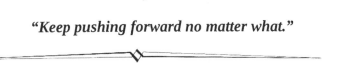

"Keep pushing forward no matter what."

Dr. King's dedication to self-care was evident in his occasional hospital admissions for comprehensive check-ups and moments of recalibration. Only those closest to him knew, as there was a negative stigma attached to mental health issues. Thus, discrediting him and hindering the civil rights movement or perhaps ending it. Instead, he took his advice, "If you can't fly, then run; if you can't run, then walk; if you can't walk, then crawl, but whatever you do, you have to keep moving forward." He kept moving forward. We can too!

Dr. King attempted suicide early in his life before the age of thirteen. Once due to insurmountable grief after the loss of his beloved grandmother, who helped raise him. While Dr. King was never officially diagnosed, some have said he experienced bouts of mental fatigue—depression. Like President Lyndon B. Johnson, who faced tremendous stress from the Vietnam War and the ongoing civil rights movement, these visionary leaders bore the weight of their respective challenges with remarkable resilience and courage. Despite holding the highest office in the land, he struggled with the burdens of leadership. Stress is a universal challenge that can afflict individuals of any race, regardless of their social status or position, and can strike at any moment. Dr. King understood that the civil rights movement's success depended on his physical, emotional, and mental well-being. His commitment to his health and well-being made him a more effective leader.

When examining a legacy, flaws may be sought, but the mission's fulfillment for humanity's betterment remains paramount.

In today's society, particularly for Black men and women, we have to prioritize self-care, health care, and mental health—without concern for external appearances or backlash. Our health and well-being are paramount, and by taking care of ourselves, we can better contribute to our communities and the causes that are meaningful to us.

I've discovered that maintaining your health is necessary, regardless of your role or position in society. Whether you're a leader in business, politics, the community, a spiritual leader, or a head of your household, your well-being is paramount. Do not overlook your health because of the expectations others place on you. It's important not to be afraid to express your needs and seek the care and support necessary to maintain good health.

Even someone revered as Dr. King, a pastor and civil rights leader, was first and foremost a human being. He recognized the importance of protecting his physical and mental well-being, understanding that self-care was paramount to being an effective leader, pastor, husband, and father.

It's important to dispel the misconception that Black men are always strong and capable of withstanding anything. Just like anyone else, Black men have vulnerabilities and face various challenges. Societal expectations and stereotypes often hinder the expression of feelings and struggles. Access to quality healthcare and socioeconomic factors also play a role in addressing health issues. Achieving a balance between strength and vulnerability and prioritizing health and self-care is crucial for everyone, regardless of their background, race, gender, or societal role.

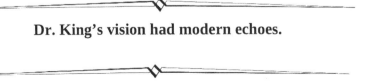

Dr. King's vision had modern echoes.

Dr. King's philosophy was deeply rooted in the teachings of Jesus Christ. Love, for him, was not just an abstract concept but a tangible force that moved and guided his actions. This love ethic was the foundation of his work. Dr. King understood that love is love. Society today, not so much. Love and hate cannot occupy the same space. If there is an increase in hate, there is a decrease in love. We teach love has to be taught, and in this society, we need to train more of it. We are ripping it apart. Minimizing its values gives room for hatred to evolve. In his teachings, he explained the concept of loving one's enemies, making it accessible and meaningful to those who may initially find it perplexing. Dr. King's ability to break down complex ideas into relatable concepts was one of his remarkable qualities.

I routinely offered my expertise and understanding of nonviolence, a credential I partly earned from the King Center in collaboration with Emory University. I was privileged to be mentored by Dr. Bernard Lafayette, a civil rights activist. Bernard Lafayette was a staff member of the SNCC and the first among the SNCC staff to lead organizing efforts to vote at the county courthouse in Selma. During one voter registration drive, he was attacked and beaten. He advocated for nonviolence before he met and worked with Dr. King, and Bernard Lafayette still taught his nonviolence philosophy.

Dr. Bernard Lafayette is known as the authority on Kingian Nonviolence. Kingian is a comprehensive approach encompassing multidiscipline, equipping individuals and communities with the knowledge and skills to resolve conflicts peacefully without violence. These trainings disclose the rich legacy of Dr. King's teachings, providing practical tools and insights for fostering harmony and understanding in various contexts based on strategies he used during the civil rights movement. He has been a nonviolent activist for more than half a century and was a close associate of Martin Luther King Jr. Lafayette says nonviolence aims to win people over by showing them love. He emphasizes, "You win them over through your behavior, character, and love for them." A person of love has the moral authority to set the standard. Dr. Lafayette states, "Don't allow people to cause you to be violent because they are violent, because violence begets violence." He says people are not evil, though they do many evil things. "But they are human beings, people with a life and grew up in different cultures. They didn't choose their families, neighborhoods, or the country they were born in. They just showed up. Their environment conditions them. Therefore, people can be unconditioned. They can change. We have to believe that people can change."

Atlanta is a beautiful city with an unbelievable history. While I lived in Atlanta, one of my initial endeavors related to Dr. King was to schedule a visit to view some of his papers. Coordinating with the head of the department, I would venture into the room housing Dr. King's vast collection of documents. There, at the King Center, I'd peruse the available catalog, jotting down the titles and numbers of documents I was interested in. Although I couldn't handle his original papers directly, the staff provided copies of my selected documents. Being so close to his writings, feeling the weight of history in every word, was an unparalleled experience. When you know the facts and have the truth in your hands, you can't help but learn. Education is key. You can be educated simply by curiosity, research, and intellectual and fact-based conversations.

Learning becomes almost inevitable when you possess accurate facts and have access to the truth. That is because we build knowledge on the foundation of facts and truth. They provide a solid framework for understanding the world around us and can stimulate curiosity and desire to obtain a more in-depth exploration of facts. That's why everything I learned held so much value. I didn't know half of what I discovered.

Knowing the facts and having access to the truth can spark critical thinking, promote informed decision-making, and inspire further inquiry. It encourages individuals to seek additional information, ask thought-provoking questions, and engage in meaningful discussions. Through this continuous learning process, people can gain a deeper and more comprehensive understanding of various subjects, from history and science to ethics and culture. Once I started this journey, I couldn't depart from it like others. I wouldn't return to the lack of accurate insight regarding our history and how it impacts our future.

In researching the life of Dr. King, along with my experiences in pursuing my education and various personal goals, I've recognized the importance of communicating accurate information. Facts and truth catalyze intellectual growth and enlightenment, empowering me to expand my knowledge and make well-informed choices in various aspects of life.

I worked with the National Park Service at Dr. King's church for several years. This experience brought me closer to history and a deeper understanding of its truth and its truth. During this time, I gave historical presentations about the church and performed re-enactments of some of Dr. King's speeches. I shadowed three to four rangers at Dr. King's birth home, recording their tours to capture little-known facts and insights. At home, I meticulously transcribed these recordings, using them to craft my own engaging and informative presentation.

I delivered the presentation at the church, during neighborhood tours, and at Fire Station #6 in Atlanta, where Dr. King played in the basement as a child and was one of the city's first integrated fire stations. However, these performances typically took place in the fellowship hall, located in the church's basement.

◇

Our collective actions will bring about the greatest impact and effect change.

◇

At the Ebenezer Baptist Church, where Dr. King's journey began with his baptism at age five, his deep connection to this spiritual haven is palpable. Here, he joined as a member, was ordained, eloquently preached, and even served briefly as a co-pastor during his student years at Morehouse College. His bond with Ebenezer continued to grow as he returned as a co- pastor alongside his father, Martin Luther King Sr., from 1960 until his untimely assassination in 1968.

The church is a tale of two buildings: the original sanctuary and its newer counterpart across Auburn Avenue. In a memorable ceremony in 1999, under the guidance of Reverend Dr. Joseph Roberts Jr., who succeeded Daddy King in 1975, the congregation made a symbolic procession from the old church to the new during a service, marking a new chapter. Today, the new sanctuary is home to the services. The older one is a museum managed by the National Park Service, a unique historical site in Georgia.

It was in the original building's basement, a location of numerous pivotal civil rights movement meetings, where I had the honor of presenting, and it was also just steps from the site of Dr. King's baptism. Now home to a stage over the former baptismal pool, this space also hosts events by various organizations.

Some organizations rent the basement for their events. One day, a group out of San Francisco rented it. Jeff Steinberg, a gentleman accompanied by approximately seventy-five students across California, was the organizer of this pilgrimage. It started in Atlanta, taking them on a ten-day tour of Dr. King's path from Atlanta to Memphis, visiting significant areas of the movement. I was up in the sanctuary because they had rented out the space downstairs. The gentleman in the group had ventured upstairs to see the sanctuary, and we organically engaged in a conversation. Once I had told him about my speaking as Dr. King downstairs, he asked if I would do some of Dr. King for them. I wanted the kids to hear Dr. King as much as possible, so I didn't refuse them.

My eyes met a woman illuminated with wisdom simply observing. Then, drawn to engage, I had an enlightening conversation with a pleasant lady uniquely well-versed in our history. She spoke of how many schools in the South refused to admit Black students, even though the 1954 *Brown v. Board of Education* Supreme Court decision decreed school segregation unconstitutional. This woman most intimately knew the horrific details, the hate, the reverberation of obscenities shouted, and what it felt to have objects hurled at them. She was one of the nine courageous Black students who, despite the verbal and physical attacks, helped desegregate public schools.

She is Minnijean Brown Trickey, one of the Little Rock Nine students at Little Rock Central High School. She integrated into the school. Minnijean Trickey was the first student expelled for retaliating against the torment. As she spoke, I wholeheartedly embraced and internalized the rich narration of history that unfolded before me.

Contemplating the impact of their actions, which have so positively shaped our future, left me utterly speechless. It prompted the question: What if our contemporary society consistently reflected on our actions? Imagine the potential if we routinely considered how our deeds could affect others, inspire or enhance someone's life, or even contribute to the betterment of society. Such introspection could lead to a more empathetic and forward-thinking community.

Whenever I listened to the wisdom of someone from the civil rights movement, it hit me that they shared the commonality of pain. It was perceived as though it had happened yesterday. In some ways, it was still present.

As we conversed, Minnijean Trickey softly and glowingly mentioned, "My favorite speech from Dr. King was the one he gave at the funeral of the four little girls killed in Birmingham's Sixteenth Street Baptist Church."

So, I started reciting it.

"These children, unoffending, innocent, and beautiful, were the victims of..." and her eyes welled with tears. Aware that it had deeply affected her, I spoke for only a bit more of Dr. King's speech and returned to the sanctuary, feeling the weight of pain in her heart.

Jeff Steinberg founded the Sojourn to the Past (Sojourn Project), which brought the group. Minnijean Brown Trickey dedicates her time to traveling and engaging with students and educators. She conducts impactful lessons on intolerance, institutional racism, and contemporary social justice issues. Drawing from her encounters with explicit racial hatred, her insights are uniquely poignant. As a lifelong activist, Minnijean Trickey can recount these experiences with remarkable clarity and perspective, offering invaluable lessons from her life's journey in the fight against racial injustice.

Jeff Steinburg returned to the sanctuary after Minnijean Trickey had spoken to him about me. She convinced Mr. Steinburg to take me on the balance of the tour, which was eight days; they had already spent two days in Atlanta. He asked me if I would be willing to go with them and "be King" the whole time, and I agreed.

It was a phenomenal experience. The students called for Dr. King to eat breakfast with them. They wanted to hear the narratives from history, messages, and lessons in his voice.

Then their tour reached the Sixteenth Street Baptist Church in Birmingham. In 1963, during the height of the civil rights movement, the Ku Klux Klan tragically bombed the church, resulting in the loss of four young girls' lives. This heartbreaking event marked a sad moment in the struggle for civil rights. They had already planned for me to recreate the eulogy from the church's pulpit. With great humility, I stood in that very pulpit, speaking as Dr. King. Not only did I give a presentation of the eulogy, but the parents and some of the family members of the four little girls were in the congregation that day.

Throughout the tour, Jeff Steinberg ensured a profoundly educational experience by arranging for individuals involved in the civil rights movement to meet us at each stop. These participants, often accompanied by family members, shared their personal stories and experiences with the students, enriching the journey with firsthand accounts of this pivotal historical period.

On a significant day in history, January 15, 2017, which marked Dr. King's eighty-eighth birthday, I had the unique opportunity to speak from behind the pulpit of both the original and the currently active Ebenezer Baptist Church. That came about thanks to Dr. McNeil, the music director at Ebenezer, who invited me to participate in a particular program they had organized.

The year prior, in 2016, I met my now manager Mrs. Hilda Willis at the Ray Charles Performing Arts Center on the campus of Morehouse College in Atlanta where I performed as King for the Black Theatre Festival. She has been a great inspiration and tremendous help in all aspects of my work with MLK.

The Turning Point

We all have a turning point in our lives when we decide where a change occurs, especially with beneficial results, ideally for the better. The goal is to be mindful of what needs to be accomplished so we can envision the new route and approach it with thought and care.

The turning point for me was realizing how little I knew about our most outstanding leader, whose words I passionately recited—cliff notes, short summaries of tremendous historical accomplishments, amounting to the same as most of the world. With time, the notes seemed to diminish from generation to generation, as if the words were fading and they no longer remembered the pain. In contrast, the generations who lived and died for that history moved us forward and silently departed without much of a trace.

I reached the turning point where I no longer wanted to merely acknowledge Dr. Martin Luther King Jr. or any other civil rights movement leaders. I wanted to know them intimately. It's impossible to walk in the shoes of giants. Still, I could follow their trails, pick up breadcrumbs of unearthed knowledge, embark on the detours they were forced to take, research the history, read informative books about their lives—the ones collecting dust—visit the places they affected change, and meet the people they encountered, marched with, fought for or died as a sacrifice for us to have a better world in which to live. I am eager to hear more intimate and personal accounts of their lives and that era firsthand. That is why I took this journey; nothing compares to it. Nothing.

Self-education is a chore. No, it is a gift. It is a way to understand the true essence of the human mind and how it *works. Gain insights into the motivations that no one knew about. It's an opportunity to fill in the holes that exist everywhere—the holes in the textbooks they want to remove. We must lend our most powerful voice to ensure they do not remove our history, as it is comparable to removing our contributions and erasing our existence in society.*

The turning point is now. We must unearth these historical treasures and share them—with everyone. But we must first work to fully understand it, respect the sacrifices to create such change, and determine our contributions moving forward. We can no longer sit by and read about the contributions of others. Society is begging us to stand up and do what needs to be done— create change most effectively. War, hate, fighting, and killing are not the answer. There has to be another way. We have the blueprint. We must raise and cultivate leaders.

Self-education is a chore. No, it is a gift. It is a way to understand the true essence of the human mind and how it works.

-from the Chapter The Turning Point

Chapter 8
The March That Changed America

A landmark event. The March on Washington for Jobs and Freedom was a pivotal event in the the civil rights movement when prominent civil rights groups and iconic figures of the era joined forces in a collaborative effort for change. The massive protest gathered an estimated 250,000 people—a broad spectrum from diverse backgrounds and regions who came together on the steps of the Lincoln Memorial in Washington, D.C. Visualize a vast assembly of individuals from diverse backgrounds, ethnicities, and hues, standing and sitting together—around the reflecting pool, denoting hope and the promise of a brighter future.

If we were to come together for measurable action, imagine the outcome. The historic March on Washington for Jobs and Freedom in 1963 had a primary purpose: advocating for civil rights and equality for African Americans. During that time we were systematically subjected to racial segregation, discrimination, and disenfranchisement in the United States. Today demands the same strength and unification to bring about the necessary change. As long as we continue to be divided, angry, and unwilling to learn about and understand our differences and similarities, we can't.

The March on Washington for Jobs and Freedom aimed to address these injustices and call for significant changes in policies and laws that perpetuated racial inequality. While substantial progress has been made since then, it's vital to recognize that racial inequality and discrimination still exist on a significant level in contemporary society. The fight for civil rights is an ongoing struggle that requires continued efforts. The need for strength and unified support stems from the fact that systemic inequalities and racial discrimination still exist.

The march addressed several critical issues, with its central demand being the passage of comprehensive civil rights legislation that would end racial segregation in public spaces, eliminate discriminatory employment practices, and safeguard the voting rights of African Americans. The organizers and participants sought to bring national attention to the pervasive racial injustices still plaguing this country.

Dr. King's call to rediscover moral and spiritual values remains relevant, emphasizing empathy and justice in addressing modern-day challenges.

The March on Washington promoted economic justice, advocating for a higher minimum wage and expanding job opportunities for African Americans. However, we must recognize that despite some progress, we have not yet reached a point where our efforts are no longer necessary. It's insufficient to evaluate our financial security and dismiss the significance of broader societal challenges. Such a perspective fails to embrace the fundamental concept of loving one another and perpetuates the persistence of racism. To address these enduring inequalities, we must work against divisive tactics and unite our collective voices and actions, viewing ourselves and others as equals.

The march also served as a response to police brutality and racial violence. We can shift the mindset of society when we come together with shared initiatives, common goals, and a unified vision. The perpetuation of systemic inequalities today directly results from our failure to establish a comprehensive structure and strategy to eliminate them.

The civil rights leaders, marchers, and speakers, with Dr. Martin Luther King Jr. at the forefront, stressed the importance of nonviolent protest and peaceful civil disobedience to achieve their objectives. Dr. King's iconic "I Have a Dream" speech during the march remains a memorable moment in the civil rights movement, underscoring the vision for a nation where their character would judge individuals rather than the color of their skin. Despite the progress, we continue to wrestle with inequalities, and indeed, we have not seen a leader like Dr. King since his time.

The Civil Rights Act of 1964 marked the commencement of deep-seated prejudices, affording us access to higher education, diverse career opportunities, and equal treatment in public domains. The 1968 Fair Housing Act reinforced a testament to the relentless struggle and shared sacrifices that granted us these hard-won legal protections. As we witness the resurgence of division and anger in our nation, we must steer society in a similar transformative direction again. Our collective strength diminishes as our divisions grow, and it remains evident that we still need to achieve equal representation in the boardrooms or in politics where pivotal decisions are made. However, a reservoir of influential decision-makers exists, with the potential to tip the scales toward balance and fairness.

The March on Washington was a significant and transformative event that aimed to draw attention to the urgent need for civil rights and racial equality in the United States. It was a powerful demonstration of solidarity and a catalyst for legislative changes that eventually led to the passage of landmark civil rights legislation, including the Civil Rights Act of 1964 and the Voting Rights Act of 1965.

A shift in our surroundings can be a catalyst for broadening our perspectives, beliefs, and understanding. The new environment exposes us to different experiences and viewpoints, prompting us to rethink and expand our own ideas.

In 1959, Dr. King traveled to India to better understand Mahatma Gandhi's nonviolent direct-action philosophy and connect more intimately with Gandhi's legacy. Drawing inspiration from Gandhi's approach to nonviolent resistance, Dr. King held that peaceful protests in the civil rights movement would be morally compelling and strategically effective. He believed such demonstrations, conducted with dignity and discipline, would capture the media's attention and sway public opinion. His strategy was rooted in the idea that nonviolent actions, highlighting the sharp contrast between the peaceful demeanor of the protestors and the brutal responses they faced, would evoke empathy and support from the wider public. This approach aimed to create a powerful narrative that could not be ignored, which led to advancing civil rights through moral and social influence.

The Anniversary of the March on Washington is a poignant reflection of the progress journey and persistent challenges.

It is heartening to witness various organizations converging for such significant events. However, it's equally disheartening to acknowledge that we're continuing to have these entrenched issues, including violence and discrimination, supporting the necessity for sustained efforts toward justice and equality.

The strength of the civil rights movement lay in its unity and inclusivity. The leaders of the march, the Big Six leaders, included prominent civil rights activists and organizations. They worked together, emphasizing the importance of togetherness—not just for a single day, but for a lifetime. Today, we need more collaboration between organizations. We're stronger together.

Dr. King's message about rediscovering lost values remains relevant. We must return to the moral and spiritual foundations that underpin our society. He said, "If we are to go forward, we must go back and rediscover these precious values—that all reality hinges on moral foundations and that all reality has spiritual control."

Pulling our collective efforts together, Dr. King's strategy was to garner media attention to shed light on the issues. However, we've got to recognize that forces aim to keep us divided, as division weakens our collective strength. It keeps us fighting and hating one another. Hate and division are brilliant distractions to progress. Just as Pharaoh sought to keep slaves fighting against themselves, those who opposed progress often employed strategies to support the division of communities. Overcoming this division is necessary for progress and unity. Examine the recent societal impacts of uniting for the exact cause.

Drawing fundamental connections to the civil rights movement resonates with today's society. It displays the critical theme of unity, emphasizing how diverse leaders united to drive the movement's success. This message remains as pertinent as ever in a divided society, urging people from various backgrounds to join for common causes. We must stay persistent in understanding that challenges such as violence, discrimination, and racial inequality signal that the struggle for civil rights is ongoing.

Dr. King's call to rediscover lost moral and spiritual values resonates deeply with today's society, where materialism and ethical dilemmas prevail. These values guide us to address today's issues with empathy and justice. We have access to the media and need to use it to raise awareness, paralleling Dr. King's strategy of leveraging the media's power to bring attention to current civil rights issues.

Our responsibility is to employ media platforms for constructive purposes, combating misinformation and hate. People must recognize that division has historically been used as a tool of oppression and not fall prey to the distractions that surround them. We can identify and resist contemporary strategies to sow discord among different groups. Unity propelled the civil rights movement. Coming together as a united front is imperative for addressing today's societal challenges.

The time I've invested in the reflection on the enduring lessons and principles of the civil rights movement and their applicability to today's world has brought unprecedented value. It has uncovered the importance of unity, moral values, and responsible media use while recognizing the ongoing civil rights and social justice struggles. Ultimately, it calls upon individuals and communities to continue the civil rights movement's legacy by fostering a more equitable and inclusive society.

Preparing to speak, I stood in the pulpit of Brown Chapel AME in 2018, commemorating Bloody Sunday, where Jesse Jackson was the keynote. The church pastor at the time was Reverend Strong. That day, he had asked me to do two or three short segments of Dr. King between other events and speakers on the program. In the pulpit, a particular gentleman, Dr. Clarence Jones, sat to the left side of me with five or six people on each side of the podium as I did an excerpt from Dr. King's "How Long, Not Long."

The conclusion of my speech was met with thunderous applause, initiating a standing ovation. When I turned around, Jesse Jackson looked at me, smiling. He told me it was great and gave me a big hug. I thanked him and sat on the podium's right side. With five or six cameras on from various television stations waiting to interview Dr. Jones, he kindly greeted me with a hug that felt like the weight and significance of that historical day. That was the first time Dr. Jones heard me speak as Dr. King. He thanked me for delivering the words of Martin Luther King Jr. and enlightened me as to who he was—Dr. Clarence B. Jones helped write many of King's speeches, including those I gave that day. Dr. Jones was Dr. King's personal attorney and draft speech writer. I was surprised to learn that he helped write the first five paragraphs of the speech to the March on Washington, "I Have a Dream."

It was hard to believe that I was standing in this historic church after speaking the words of Dr. King, conversing with his attorney on the pulpit.

Adjusting his eyeglasses, Dr. Jones confessed, "Had I not seen with my own eyes and heard you with my own ears, had somebody just given me a voice recording, I'd say, well, that's Martin Luther King Jr. But when I saw you and heard you speak his words, it was an out-of-body experience. Particularly when you quoted that part, 'How Long.'" He shook his head in disbelief and continued, "I remember the circumstances. You do a service to his memory and to our movement. To whatever extent you can use your gift to capture the authenticity of his voice—it's not just the authenticity, but the tremor. It's almost scary. It's painful for me, quite honestly. It's painful to sit there. I had to sort of clutch myself." He went on to explain that God told him to enjoy it. "This man has been given an unexpected gift."

Dr. Jones is a man with great humility. I've read his books *The Making of the Dream* and *What Would King Say*, had valuable conversations, and learned facts and details from Dr. Jones outside the books. About a year later, Dr. Jones invited me to speak at a function he sponsored in Sunnylands—Rancho Mirage, California. I was honored to be part of it.

Dr. Clarence Jones had an intimately close relationship with Dr. Martin Luther King Jr. Living alongside him, Dr. Jones was not just an associate but a confidant and collaborator. In a significant demonstration of this bond, Dr. Jones crafted the handwritten proposed text for Dr. King's speeches upon Dr. King's request. This text culminated their discussions over the preceding five weeks, reflecting a deep understanding and synthesis of their shared ideas and visions. As Dr. King spoke during the March on Washington for Jobs and Freedom on August 28, 1963, Dr. Clarence Jones listened to every word, realizing that he used the first seven paragraphs of what he suggested verbatim without changing a single sentence. When Dr. Jones saw a copy of the speech, Dr. King seamlessly added his paragraphs after the first seven paragraphs of the opening. As he spoke, Mahalia Jackson, the greatest and most influential gospel singer of that time, shouted, "Tell them about the dream, Martin! Tell them about the dream!"

Once Mahalia Jackson shouted that, Dr. Jones, just fifty feet behind him, said Dr. King began to speak. People remember and celebrate the balance of the speech: "Extemporaneous and spontaneous." He only talked about the dream near the end of the speech. It is as if some cosmic transcendental force came down and took over Martin Luther King Jr.'s body that day. Same body, same voice. Same everything, except not."

Indeed, Dr. Martin Luther King Jr. has been paid many eloquent tributes, and Dr. Clarence Jones's characterization of him is particularly poignant. When Dr. Jones described Dr. King as "the preeminent apostle of nonviolence, love, and commitment to excellence," he captured the essence of Dr. King's enduring legacy beautifully and profoundly. This statement succinctly encapsulates the core principles Dr. King championed and lived by, making it a fitting homage to his extraordinary life and work.

We must continue to address and resolve internal challenges within our communities and between others.

Achieving the next level of impact in addressing today's systemic inequalities requires a multifaceted approach. It begins with a comprehensive grasp of our history, delving deep into the political motivations that have shaped our society. We must gain a more factual understanding of the issues to move forward. Collaboration becomes crucial, as organizations must unite their efforts and work together toward a common goal. Nonviolence should be our guiding principle, coupled with an unwavering passion fueled by a clear purpose and steadfast commitment to the desired results. This strategy is not merely a blueprint for the past but a relevant roadmap for addressing contemporary societal challenges.

Education is a powerful tool in addressing social conflict and promoting reconciliation. By encouraging understanding and empathy through education, we can work toward eliminating the root causes of hatred and prevent it from further divisiveness. It's crucial to remain hopeful and proactive in our efforts. While some individuals propagate hate more effectively than those who promote love, we have a historical precedent from the 1960s that shows positive change can be achieved. We have to be willing to apply those same principles today to combat hatred and not allow it to become septic or go unchallenged. Inaction can inadvertently support negative actions, so being proactive in pursuing justice, equality, and unity is indispensable.

Before addressing broader societal issues, we must focus on ourselves and our communities. Sometimes, we hinder our progress. While the media may highlight specific incidents, this self-destructive behavior is prevalent in various communities nationwide. A prime example is the violence in Chicago, where we see members of our community killing or harming one another. We must start by cleaning up our front yards to create meaningful change. Change begins at home, within our communities, and by addressing these internal challenges, we can better equip ourselves to tackle more extensive societal issues.

"I have a dream that one day on the red hills of Georgia, the sons of former slaves and the sons of former slave owners will be able to sit down together at a table of brotherhood."
Dr. Martin Luther King Jr.

Dr. King's "I Have a Dream" speech remains an enduring masterpiece of 20th-century oratory, transcending the bounds of time and resonating with immense power today. Delivered in a historic moment, the "I Have a Dream" speech radiated across the nation, captivating an audience that spanned racial and social divides. Broadcast live on television, Dr. King's words, spoken over sixteen minutes, left an indelible mark on millions, etching the importance of his message deep into the collective consciousness. Please take the time to read his remarkable address. The realization of Dr. King's dream began to take shape relatively quickly, particularly on the legislative front.

Following a decade of relentless advocacy led by organizations like the NAACP and sustained peaceful protests for civil rights, President Lyndon Johnson signed the Civil Rights Act of 1964 into law. He furthered this progress a year later by signing the National Voting Rights Act. These legislative milestones were vital steps toward achieving equality and justice for all. Dr. King's unwavering belief in peaceful protest as a catalyst for change endowed his cause with unparalleled moral authority. His approach shifted the spotlight from conflicts to the underlying issues, emphasizing the power of nonviolence to drive meaningful progress. Some are unaware that Dr. King's advocacy extended beyond the African American community;

he championed the rights of all oppressed individuals. He did that for us and future generations. His philosophical understanding that injustice anywhere threatened justice everywhere defined his leadership. Dr. King's inclusive vision, transcending boundaries and divisions, is a timeless example and vital imperative in today's fractured world.

Stepping into Greatness Channeling Dr. King's Legacy

When I step into the imprint of Dr. King's footprints, I'm overwhelmed by an acute sense of humility and unworthiness. It's an enormous responsibility to embody such a towering figure—a historical giant. The nervousness and butterflies persist until I begin speaking, as I strive to imagine the essence of King, his discussions with Coretta, and his purpose. I dress meticulously in a black or blue suit and tie, mirroring Dr. King's crisp and polished appearance. It's not about where or what I'm speaking about; the anxiety stems from the weight of representing him, knowing I must do justice to Reverend Dr. Martin Luther King Jr.

Once I begin, it's as if Dr. King takes over when I open my mouth. The energy becomes palpable, and I feel his presence right beside me. The audience's reactions are astonishing; their eyes widen, mouths fall agape, and they stare in disbelief. It's as if I've transported myself back to 1965, experiencing the era as it was. Speaking as Dr. King feels like opening my mouth, and he is the one speaking through me. The connection with the audience is electric, but I'm acutely aware that there's no comparing myself to this remarkable man and the enduring impact he had and continues to have on the world.

As the speaking engagement concludes, applause fills the room, reporters approach with questions, and some even inquire if I'm an actor in a movie about Dr. King. The older generation, *who lived through that era and perhaps even participated in the March on Washington, approached me with astonishment and nostalgia. Some say, "I was at the March. I swear when I came in here, I said to myself, this man has come back." They often share heartfelt stories and experiences, and their emotions sometimes bring tears to their eyes. They knew a reality that we, the younger generation, can only read about, and I, in my portrayal, am a humble reminder of that pivotal time. I'm just reloading history's voice from the past and touching hearts.*

Chapter 9
Bridging Generations

U nderstanding our history is paramount for all individuals, regardless of their background. It's an invaluable guide for our journey forward, offering lessons and insights particularly relevant in today's complex world. History connects to our roots, reminding us of our origins and shaping our collective identity. It gives us the most precious opportunity to impart this knowledge to future generations, ensuring that the legacy endures—it's never forgotten. We risk losing a vital thread in our society if we neglect this responsibility.

We must be willing to engage in open, respectful, and active communication with individuals from different generations. We must listen, understand their perspectives, and express our viewpoints clearly.

As stated in his final book, Dr. King asked, "Where do we go from here?" It's a question that continues to echo through the corridors of time, demanding answers from each generation, taking us beyond the dream. To contribute meaningfully to this ongoing dialogue, I recognized the need to immerse myself in the wealth of information, resources, and knowledge. I embarked on a personal journey, much like Dr. King's march, seeking to connect with the sheer soil and atmosphere that shaped his mission, all while safe from the dangers he faced.

Given I worked closely with the National Park Service (The Martin Luther King Jr. National Historical Park), and they knew me, I called The King Center and asked about access to the King Library and Archives, which provided me with an invaluable opportunity to study the rich repository of historical materials. It's home to the most extensive primary source materials for Dr. Martin Luther King Jr. and the global civil rights movement. As I engaged with this remarkable resource, I couldn't help but feel a sense of reverence. I found the keys to unlocking a deeper understanding of Dr. King's legacy among these meticulously preserved documents. We possess access to far more than we actively seek or utilize.

Access to this treasure trove of historical accuracy allowed me to connect with Dr. King on a more personal level. It was a privilege to peruse copies of his sermons, letters, speeches, and various writings. Each of these documents offered a glimpse into Dr. King's intimate thoughts, ideas, and emotions, bringing me closer to the essence of the man himself. It was a humbling experience to hold the pages that once bore the weight of his visionary words and commitment to justice and equality. As I was self-educating, I embraced the power of our history. This endeavor allowed me to understand his unwavering dedication to the betterment of humanity. Having acquired a more bottomless well of knowledge than ever taught, I've realized that sharing Dr. King's speeches isn't just about passing on words, it's about imparting his insights. That is especially true for the younger generation today, many of whom might need to familiarize themselves with the most outstanding leader of our time. Witnessing the impression of Dr. King's wisdom on their faces and eyes filled me with hope to inspire them to take meaningful action. It left me contemplating the transformative potential of our world today if Dr. King were still among us.

We must dare to understand Dr. King's vision for humanity and act on it.

Historical knowledge can continue to play a role in society if we know and understand it. Dr. Martin Luther King Jr.'s beliefs provide a timeless bridge between generations of African Americans and the broader culture—a nonviolent awakening. His core principles of justice, equality, and nonviolence resonate across time, offering a unifying communication that binds us together. By embracing Dr. King's vision, we create a shared heritage that transcends age and background, suggesting a common ground for dialogue and action.

Dr. King's legacy is a source of inspiration and a call to activism for the younger generation. His courageous stand against injustice and his commitment to peaceful change motivate young people to engage in contemporary struggles for civil rights, racial equality, and social justice. His words remind them that they, too, can be agents of change, just as he was. For the older generation, Dr. King's beliefs evoke memories of the civil rights movement and the transformative power of collective action. They link to their experiences and struggles, reinforcing the importance of persistence and resilience in adversity. This connection between generations strengthens the resolve to continue the fight for equality and justice.

By embracing Dr. King's beliefs and values, we create a bridge that spans generations and closes the distance between history and action, nurturing understanding, empathy, and a shared commitment to creating a more just and equitable society. It reminds us that the struggle for civil rights isn't a relic of the past but an ongoing journey that requires the collective efforts of all generations working together.

Dr. King's lifelong dedication to serving others is a deep-rooted contrast to current growing individualism. His emphasis on communal responsibility and self-sacrifice is a reminder of the values that seem to be diminishing. To reverse this trend, we must collectively rekindle a sense of empathy and commitment towards one another. It's still possible, but it requires a concerted effort to prioritize the common good over individual interests. This shift can be achieved through education, encouraging a sense of community, and daily supporting acts of kindness and compassion. Dr. King's legacy reminds us that working toward a more inclusive and selfless society is never too late. We must boldly grasp Dr. King's vision for humanity and translate it into action.

Yesterday can help us navigate today's challenges and inspire action in a complex world.

For nine years, I genuinely enjoyed residing in Atlanta, a city deeply intertwined with the history of the civil rights movement and Dr. Martin Luther King, Jr. I was drawn to the significance of this place, Dr. King's baptism site at Ebenezer Baptist Church and his and Coretta Scott King's final resting place.

It was a location that held profound historical importance, and I was perplexed by the apparent desensitization of many people to this fact. It troubled me that some residents of Atlanta, who had lived there for their entire lives, had never taken the opportunity to visit the King Center or fully engage with this rich history.

My experience reciting Dr. King's speeches compelled me to take a journey of discovery, and it was turning into one that would lead me deeper into an era I had not fully comprehended during my younger years. We know the basics. The holiday, the march, "I Have a Dream," but little else. It became increasingly clear that this path wasn't a choice. I was on the way to my destiny. It's a calling placed upon my life.

In the underground chambers of the Ebenezer Baptist Church, I had the privilege of delivering historical presentations and immersive reenactments of Dr. King's effective speeches and sermons. Fondly referred to as the basement, this hallowed space within the church, also known as the fellowship hall, where congregants convened for meals and meetings, now stands as a celebrated institution under the stewardship of the National Park Service, adorned with the iconic blue Ebenezer sign. For nearly eight decades, from 1922 to 1999, this consecrated venue bore witness to countless services.

In 1999, the church transitioned to a new location across Auburn Avenue. I continued my mission of enlightenment and education in the Fellowship Hall until 2019, concluding my endeavors just months before the onset of the global pandemic.

The basement, steeped in historical significance, served as the canvas upon which I orally painted portraits of Dr. King's life and work, disseminating knowledge, and fostering appreciation for his prevailing legacy. Positioned at the heart of the MLK National Historic Park, which draws approximately one million visitors worldwide annually, I dedicated three to five days a week for seven years to this endeavor.

During the final four years of this remarkable journey, I made my home just a block away from the church on Auburn Avenue, right across from the hallowed grounds of Dr. King's birth. This proximity facilitated a seamless, three-minute stroll across Auburn and Boulevard to my workplace daily, with a view of the church's steeple gracing my front porch.

In that basement, my passion for propagating the teachings of Dr. King flourished. A testament to the power of this setting, approximately 75% of my speaking and performance engagements during that period were the result of individuals who witnessed my presentations in this sacred space.

Disheartening, yes, but it's a sobering reality to contemplate the ongoing struggle for basic rights, particularly the fundamental right to vote and equality. Voting isn't just our civic duty; it's the cornerstone of democracy. It's a choice. Power. Change. Justice. Balance. Freedom. Understanding our history, particularly the historical suffrage and sacrifices made, only amplifies the frustration and disappointment that not every eligible citizen exercises this right.

***

Our history is fraught with battles for equal access to the ballot, with individuals fighting against discrimination, disenfranchisement, and even violence to secure this right.

***

The stories of those who came before us and the sacrifices they endured should remind us of the significance of our right to vote. It's a right that all eligible citizens should cherish, respect, and exercise. Through this democratic process, we have the power to shape the course of our nation, advocate for change, and ensure the upholding of principles of justice and equality. are upheld. The civil rights movement gave us that and other rights that we must place in the highest priority of our lives. Voting. Nonviolence. Peace. Love.

The fact that only some people exercise these right stresses the need for continued education and awareness about the importance of voting. It's a reminder that the struggle for civil rights and social justice is ongoing and that we must remain vigilant and committed to upholding the principles of democracy for the betterment of society. Leave the imprint of your voice. The idea that anyone, regardless of their background, race, or beliefs, would have to fight for a right they were born with is a painful reminder of the historical injustices many have faced.

The struggles of the past, including the civil rights movement, remind us that progress is not guaranteed and that we must remain actively engaged in the ongoing fight for equality and justice. By respecting and exercising our right to vote, we can amplify our voices and work toward a more inclusive and equitable future—for all. Imagine what this world would look like today if we didn't have that right. We must be more vigilant in protecting these rights and ensuring they are accessible to all. Voting isn't just a privilege; it's a responsibility and means by which we can shape the direction of our society.

Over the past twenty years, I have dedicated myself to answering this divine call, committed to preserving and sharing the legacy of Dr. King and the civil rights movement.

It's a journey that's allowed me to connect with the spirit of this history and pass on its lessons and significance to present and future generations, ensuring that the powerful message of justice, equality, and social change lives on.

Our life is valuable, and we must stand for something meaningful and purposeful to leave a legacy of change.

A Call to Contemplate Our Impact

n June of 2020, during the tumultuous COVID-19 pandemic, I found myself back in Fayetteville, having put my presentations at the Martin Luther King Jr. National Historical Park on hold toward the end of the summer of 2019. Then, everything shut down. At first, this pause left me devastated by the tremendous loss of life and how everything still became. But as time unfolded, I began to discern a higher purpose in the trajectory of my life. It became clear that God had orchestrated the hiatus from performing.

During this period of reflection, my mind wasn't idle. I had years to learn and time to process my experiences, the research, the conversations, and the education I received. I had absorbed Dr. King's words' greatness, intent, and why behind some of his motivations.

I didn't feel fraudulent in reciting his words. Given the honor bestowed upon me by Dr. King's estate, who granted me the legal right to share his words, I felt a tremendous responsibility not to disappoint them. I aspired to impart knowledge, especially to our younger generation, about Dr. King and the challenges of the civil rights movement, with the hope that they would gain insights and feel empowered to carry forward the mission for justice and equality, extending their advocacy to encompass all of God's children.

We must invest the time and effort in every endeavor to fathom the underlying "why."

We possess the remarkable capacity to shape our identity and leave a lasting impact during our lifetime, but how often do we genuinely contemplate our purpose and the legacy we wish to create? If more of us took this introspective journey, the world would be markedly different. Ultimately, our accountability for our choices and how we live our lives will either become our enduring legacy or define us in a manner that shows we failed to discover or fulfill our purpose. It's a solemn and empowering realization that reveals the importance of intention, understanding, and the conscious pursuit of a meaningful life.

Our choices and actions have lasting impacts, shaping our lives and the world around us. Accountability for these choices is paramount because it determines the legacy we leave behind. When we live with intention and understanding, consciously striving for a meaningful life, we're more likely to leave a positive and enduring legacy. This legacy reflects our success in discovering and fulfilling our purpose as Dr. King and those of the civil rights era have done.

Conversely, if we fail to live thoughtfully and purposefully, we risk being defined by a legacy of unfulfilled potential or negative impact. That can reflect missed opportunities to influence our surroundings and positively contribute to the greater good.

Realizing our power to shape our legacy is both sobering and empowering. It highlights the importance of every decision we make and action we take. This understanding encourages us to live with a sense of responsibility, be mindful of how our lives affect others, and actively pursue goals that fulfill us personally and contribute positively to society.

This truth about accountability and legacy inspires us to live more consciously. Understanding that the mark we leave on the world results from how we live our lives.

Chapter 10
Democracy's Fragile Chain is the Missing Vote

I magine what this world would look like today if we didn't have the right to vote. Just take a moment and imagine it. When we contemplate a world where this crucial democratic right is absent, we are compelled to envision a relatively unpleasant reality. Self-governance would be under threat, and the consequences would be far-reaching. The inability to vote would have a domino effect.

In such a world, the intrinsic nature of representative democracy crumbles, leaving a void where the voices and choices of African Americans once resided, excluding entire segments of society from the political process. Marginalized groups, such as minorities, women, and young people, would have no means to voice their concerns or advocate for their interests. That would result in a severe lack of representation in government.

The absence of voting rights would lead to a system dominated by a privileged few who hold power indefinitely. Policies that benefit the wealthy and powerful would be prioritized, exacerbating economic and social inequality. Social progress and justice would stagnate.

The inability to vote would have a domino effect—

cascading and interconnected consequences resulting from denying the fundamental right to vote. In essence, this single denial of a democratic right would set off a chain reaction of adverse outcomes that reverberate throughout society.

A world without the right to vote could easily slide into authoritarianism. Governments could become less accountable to the people, eroding civil liberties and curtailing freedoms of speech, assembly, and the press.

The ability to vote is a peaceful way to express our discontent with government policies. Without it, dissent could manifest in more disruptive and potentially violent ways, leading to social unrest and instability.

There would be global repercussions. Democracies around the world would lose inspiration, making it easier for authoritarian regimes to consolidate power and undermine human rights. Elected officials would not be accountable to their constituents through elections, making it easier for corruption and abuse of power to go unchecked.

The absence of diverse voices in the decision-making process would lead to policies that don't reflect the needs and aspirations of the entire population. That could lead to better informed and effective governance.

The domino effect is that voting isn't just an isolated action but a linchpin that holds together the broader framework of democracy. When a segment of the population cannot exercise their right to vote, it disrupts the entire system of representation and governance. This disruption can lead to various detrimental consequences, such as unequal representation, disenfranchisement of marginalized groups, policy decisions that favor the powerful, and an erosion of the democratic principles upon which modern societies are built.

In a broader context, the concept of a "domino effect" is a compelling argument for the importance of protecting and expanding voting rights, as it emphasizes that the consequences of restricting this proper extend far beyond the act of voting itself, our democratic systems, and society as a whole.

Working together for a shared vision made the movement move.

Bridging generations from the civil rights movement to today and inspiring collective action, mainly through nonviolence, is a crucial endeavor and possible. We have to start by educating younger generations about the history of the civil rights movement, its leaders, and the principles of nonviolence. Schools, community organizations, and families can play a pivotal role in passing down this knowledge. Encourage open discussions about the struggles and achievements of that era.

All people are created equal is a principle as relevant today as it was decades ago. Regardless of our differences, we all have and must exercise the right to vote. We cannot leave it to others to speak our conscience. Our vote—every vote— and every voice matters because it can lead to the change we need.

This equality transcends mere acknowledgment; it demands active participation. The right to vote is a constitutional provision and a sacred duty. It is the voice through which we articulate our collective conscience, and it must resonate with the clarity and strength of conviction. Every vote casts a ripple, contributing to the change that shapes our society. It's robust evidence that everyone, regardless of their differences, is an integral part of the democratic process.

By placing the civil rights movement in its relevance today, we aren't solely paying homage to a pivotal chapter in history;

we also rekindle its spirit in the present. This perspective allows us to draw parallels, learn from past triumphs and setbacks, and apply these lessons to today's challenges. It's a reminder that the journey toward equality and justice is ongoing. It didn't end with Dr. King, who gave us more reason to continue his legacy. Each generation plays a role in clearing a path toward a more equitable and peaceful world. Far more significant than what we see today. That is more than history; it's a legacy that inspires, challenges, and guides us forward. Allow this to put the civil rights movement into perspective—into our consciousness.

An Intimate Glimpse of Dr. King

Frequently, we find ourselves reluctant to embark on the less-traveled path. It's often uncharted, not as smooth, and seemingly less efficient than the well-trodden alternatives. However, a potential pitfall lies in choosing the more accessible and streamlined route: the core message and lessons can become condensed or oversimplified. When a message's full depth and meaning are lost or diluted, it compromises the intended learning experience.

In my research journey, I consciously chose the longer, more contemplative, and immersive path into the life of Dr. King. While it spanned several years, it pales compared to the depth of knowledge acquired and intimate glimpse of Dr. King by his family, close associates, historians, pastors, and scholars. Nevertheless, my endeavor proved transformative, humbling, and an unparalleled source of lifelong education. Indeed, I gleaned profound insights by meticulously examining Dr. King's speeches, which I often recited at events.

My connection to Dr. King's legacy extended beyond research. I lived in a shotgun house across the street from his birthplace for seven years. I retraced the footsteps of the civil rights march on multiple occasions. I performed the iconic "I Have a Dream" speech for Time Magazine's Virtual Reality Project, lent my voice to the Godfather of Harlem series, and produced The Dream Lives Stage Play, among numerous other endeavors. None of these experiences would have materialized if I had not embraced my destiny, *followed my innate curiosity, and devoted years to research and diligent work.*

Ultimately, I recognized that my calling to become a minister was an unwavering destiny I could neither alter nor resist. I discovered this by taking the road less traveled, loaded with all kinds of gems and subtle revelations!

Chapter 11
Revelatory Reflections and
Narratives That Influence

A genuine passion for a particular subject can unlock a world of uncharted possibilities, pushing the boundaries of what one might have previously deemed unattainable. My foray into the realm of research, specifically centered on the life and legacy of Dr. King, initially sprang from a deeply personal desire to comprehend his influence on our world through his speeches. Little did I anticipate that this intellectual odyssey would lead me down paths, presenting unique opportunities to forge connections with esteemed historians, gain personal insights from Dr. King's own family, and acquire invaluable knowledge. The narratives were illuminating and evolving from one person to the next. Our history is priceless. We have to care to understand it—to feel it—and breathe in the pain, if just for a moment.

Foremost among these scholars is Clayborne Carson, whose work has played a pivotal role in shaping my comprehension of this iconic figure. This experience has only deepened my resolve to educate future generations further and encourage them to continue Dr. King's important work of love, peace, and nonviolence. Make no mistake: The world is still hungry for Dr. King's words, and we must ensure that younger generations are hungry for him.

Dr. Clayborne Carson is a prominent figure among the luminaries I have had the privilege of engaging with. As the Centennial Professor of History and Emeritus at Stanford University, Dr. Carson has dedicated his illustrious career to studying and researching Dr. Martin Luther King Jr. and the broader human rights movements inspired by visionaries like Dr. King and Mohandas K. Gandhi. His reputation as an international Martin Luther King Jr. historian is well-earned, underscored by his monumental undertaking in 1985 when Coretta Scott King entrusted him with the massive task of editing all of Dr. King's works.

This monumental effort resulted in seven volumes encapsulating Dr. King's speeches, sermons, telegrams, notes, other correspondence, and a trove of previously unpublished writings. Dr. Carson's influence extends beyond the printed page; he has lectured in over a dozen countries and played a pivotal role in the design of the national memorial honoring Dr. King. Notably, thanks to Dr. Carson's dedicated work, *The Autobiography of Martin Luther King, Jr.* exists, crafted from Dr. King's own words. Dr. Carson is also the mastermind behind the King Encyclopedia, a critical resource I may not have discovered had I not embarked on my research journey.

One particularly advantageous encounter occurred in Selma during my tour, tracing Dr. King's path from Atlanta to Memphis. I inquired about a particular book in the museum's bookstore beyond the iconic Edmund Pettus Bridge leading to Montgomery. The store attendant informed me that *The Martin Luther King, Jr. Encyclopedia* was their last copy based on extensive research written by Dr. Clayborne Carson. Without hesitation, I acquired it, recognizing the rare opportunity it presented.

Our history is rich with metamorphic moments, stories that alter perspectives and the course of our existence.

Throughout history, significant and transformative moments have changed how we view the world, impacting the direction of our lives and society. Their ability often characterizes these moments to shift our perspectives, beliefs, and actions.

My journey has allowed me to collaborate with Dr. Carson on several meaningful projects. I had the privilege of completing both Martin Luther King Jr. courses offered by Stanford University under his guidance. Dr. Carson graciously invited me to speak at Stanford during the 50th anniversary commemoration of Dr. King's assassination. This multi-day event included the recitation of Dr. King's final speech, "I've Been to the Mountaintop," precisely fifty years after its original delivery, hosted at the King Institute on the Stanford campus. Later, I repeated the performance at the university's theater, where Dr. King himself had spoken in 1967, delivering his powerful speech, "The Other America," in which he sharply delineated the division within the nation.

In Atlanta, another fortuitous encounter introduced me to the remarkable Dr. Albert Brinson, a man with solid connections to the King family and an enduring closeness to them. We crossed paths at the Greater Piney Grove Baptist Church in Atlanta, where I served as an associate minister under the esteemed Senior Pastor, Reverend Dr. William E. Flippin Sr. During a women's Sunday event, Dr. Angela Farris Watkins, Dr. King's niece and daughter of Dr. King's only sister, was the featured speaker. Dr. Flippin, keen on sharing my speaking abilities, ensured I had a place in the program.

Following the service, I received a warm thank you for my presentation. Dr. Brinson began sharing captivating stories of his close relationship with Dr. King on this occasion. In a gracious gesture, he invited me to his home, an invitation I eagerly accepted. A month later, I found myself at his residence on a tranquil Saturday morning, embarking on an enlightening journey of exploration. Dr. Brinson regaled me with captivating accounts while unveiling remarkable photographs. He captured intimate moments from Dr. King's life, many hidden from the public eye and likely destined to remain so.

Subsequently, I served alongside Dr. Brinson on the Board of Directors for the A.D. King Foundation. Through tireless efforts, he conducts informative tours of the church and various sites connected to Dr. King's legacy, including the iconic birth home.

Through my research, I have been privy to these lesser-known stories, shared laughter, and gained priceless insights into the life and contributions of one of the world's most outstanding leaders.

Chapter 12
Something To Consider

We must be willing to take pride and interest in educating ourselves on our history, the true history of America, and the issues we face. When we know America's true history and—our history—we will better understand this nation in which we live and how we got to where we are. When we know *who* we are, we have a greater sense of self-worth and understand our responsibility to our ancestors, families, and each other.

Understanding the issues and their root gives us a better roadmap. It's necessary to realize that they're the same issues. Whatever we have done to correct them isn't how we need it to be. We need the results to be adapted in a broader context and more widespread. We must examine more closely what worked. What caused the Supreme Court to render the decision that segregation on public transportation was unconstitutional? What caused Congress to pass the Civil Rights Bill? What caused Congress to pass the Voting Rights Bill the next year? Determination, commitment, and togetherness. Fifty thousand individuals united in a peaceful act of defiance, opting not to ride the city buses for 381 days. This collective action had a significant financial impact, directly affecting the revenue of the bus system. A quarter of a million people gathered at the National Mall sixty years ago; an estimated fifty thousand were white—growth, progress, compassion, and understanding.

When thousands of people started marching from Selma to Montgomery, demanding the right to vote for Black citizens, less than five months later, the Voting Rights Act was signed into law.

Together, we can move mountains—we have moved mountains.

Imagine a society where the deliberate dismantling of racist and discriminatory practices becomes the norm. In this transformed world, each step taken to eradicate bias and inequality sows the seeds for a landscape of widespread equality.

Education is paramount reimagining all educational systems as platforms to teach diversity and inclusivity. Curricula would teach history and literature from diverse perspectives and encourage critical thinking about social justice and equity. That would cultivate a generation of individuals aware of past injustices and equipped to recognize and challenge systemic biases daily.

In the workplace, removing discriminatory practices would mean going beyond tokenistic measures to ensure accurate representation and equal opportunities for *all* rather than for *some*. That could manifest in fair hiring practices, transparent promotion paths, and equitable pay structures. Work environments would become melting pots of diverse ideas and perspectives, leading to more innovative and inclusive outcomes.

A bias-free approach would ensure everyone receives the same care regardless of background. That could drastically reduce health disparities and lead to a healthier population. By actively working to eliminate racial and socioeconomic inequality, policymakers would contribute to a society where one's health and well-being are not predetermined by race or economic status.

In the justice system, fairness would be essential. Laws and policies would be scrutinized and reformed to eliminate racial bias, ensuring justice is genuinely impartial. That could lead to a significant reduction in incarceration rates among minority communities and a more rehabilitative, rather than punitive, approach to justice.

In the broader societal context, media and popular culture would play a pivotal role in shaping perceptions and attitudes. By continuing to portray and celebrate more diverse narratives and challenging stereotypes, media can help normalize inclusivity and diversity in everyday life. These concerted efforts would lead to a society where equality is not just an ideal or thought but a lived reality. This broad and systemic approach to dismantling racism and discrimination would create a world where every individual, regardless of race, has the opportunity to thrive and contribute to a more prosperous, diverse community.

One place to begin is with media. The media should be neutral. Unbiased. We are sharing the truth. Yet, that is only sometimes the case. The shared media and perspective can be perceived positively or negatively, bringing about constructive or destructive opinions and further perpetuating biases, racism, and division. It depends on how we perceive it and react.

In most cases, the reality is that media determines a person's identity, who they are, and who they become. Media influences how we think, as it's often used to paint a picture that appears through the lens of the media outlet's owner. Still, the problem arises when the narrative and perspective are false or tainted by one's beliefs. Media frames their stories in a way that tells us what to think about, how to think about it, and even sometimes what to do about it, which affects behavior.

We understand that segregation, separation, and division have been a ploy to keep the wealthy in power and the poor powerless. Knowing the facts allows us to strongly denounce the false narratives that pit us against each other and find ways to unite regardless of our differences. We form a Populist Movement 2.0. We create the love movement. We galvanize a nonpartisan love force full of people from all walks of life committed to justice, freedom, and equality for all.

We ensure that all laws are just by eliminating or changing unjust laws. When Rosa Parks asked the officer who was arresting her for refusing to give up her seat, "Why are you doing this?" his response was, "I don't know, but it's the law." As Dr. King stated, there *are* two types of laws: just and unjust. Until we eradicate injustice from society, we must continue to work to effect change. "Any law that uplifts human personality is just. Any law that degrades human personality is unjust." I believe in civil disobedience to arouse people's consciousness of persisting injustices. We all have a moral and legal responsibility to obey just laws.

Conversely, we have a moral responsibility to disobey unjust laws. "An individual who breaks a law that conscience tells him is unjust, and willingly accepts the penalty of imprisonment to arouse the conscience of the community over its injustice, is, in reality, expressing the highest respect for the law," Dr. King wrote from jail in Birmingham. Rosa greatly respected just law when she broke an unjust Jim Crow law.

What steps can we take today to ignite meaningful societal change? How can we inspire and nurture a widespread embrace of nonviolent behaviors within our society? We can create opportunities for intergenerational dialogue and engagement. Encourage young people to research individuals who were active during the civil rights movement. Hearing firsthand accounts and experiences can be incredibly meaningful and inspiring.

Promote the importance of nonviolent conflict resolution in schools and communities. Teach young people to address issues peacefully, engage in respectful dialogue, and work toward constructive solutions. Nonviolent communication workshops can be valuable.

Encourage young people to engage in community service and activism. Volunteer work, social justice projects, and advocacy campaigns can provide practical experiences working toward positive change.

Leverage digital media and storytelling platforms to share the narratives of the civil rights movement. Create documentaries, podcasts, and social media campaigns that highlight the stories of activists and their commitment to nonviolence.

Offer nonviolent training programs and workshops for young activists. Teach them the strategies and tactics of nonviolent protest, civil disobedience, and peaceful resistance. Emphasize the power of unity and solidarity.

Establish mentorship programs where experienced activists from the civil rights era mentor and guide younger activists. That can provide valuable insights, strategies, and emotional support.

Organize peaceful marches, protests, and demonstrations that echo the spirit of the civil rights movement. These events can serve as a powerful symbol of unity and a platform for advocating change.

Use art, music, and cultural events to bridge generational gaps and convey the message of nonviolence. Artistic expressions have the potential to inspire and mobilize people across age groups.

Encourage advocacy for policy changes that address

contemporary civil rights, social justice, and equality issues. Show how nonviolent activism can be an effective tool for influencing policy decisions.

Combining these strategies can promote a deeper understanding of the civil rights movement's legacy, encourage nonviolent principles, and inspire today's generations to take meaningful action for a more just and equitable society. Nonviolence remains a powerful and relevant approach to addressing social injustices and advancing the cause of civil rights.

It is an unfinished journey, and together, we can continue the legacy.

Expanding on Dr. King's assertion about the existence of just and unjust laws, its relevance to contemporary society, especially concerning the experiences of Black people and the broader population, remains significant. We can unveil subtle injustices and create a course correction by working together.

For African American communities today, the remnants of unjust laws, though not as explicit as during the era of segregation, still manifest in various forms—systemic inequalities in criminal justice, education, housing, and employment. Unjust laws in the past explicitly marginalized African Americans. Today, injustice is often more subtle, embedded in policies and practices that disproportionately affect these communities.

Dr. King's call to action remains pertinent today, urging lasting social change. It's not just about repealing overtly discriminatory laws but also about challenging and changing the systems and structures that continue to perpetuate inequality and bias. The path to true equality will occur as long as we continuously address systemic disparities today. That involves examining laws and policies to identify and rectify any elements contributing to racial disparity.

For society, this perspective extends beyond racial lines. It encompasses all forms of injustice embedded in legal and societal frameworks, whether based on gender, sexual orientation, religion, or socioeconomic status. The goal is to create an equitable society where laws and policies uphold the dignity and rights of every individual.

Continuing Dr. King's work means advocating for reform where injustice is identified, educating about the impact of these injustices, and actively participating in democratic processes to effect change. It also involves individual actions in everyday life, such as challenging prejudice, supporting equality initiatives, and promoting inclusive practices.

In essence, Dr. King's statement—and life's work—is a reminder that the journey toward justice and equality is ongoing. It's a call to remain committed to identifying, challenging, and eradicating blatant and covert unjust laws and practices, ensuring that all individuals' rights and dignities, particularly those historically marginalized, are respected and upheld.

We must explore and respect the legacy of our civil rights pioneers.

My journey has been remarkable, taking me across the globe and allowing me to meet and learn from many leaders of the civil rights era. These individuals, who walked alongside Dr. Martin Luther King Jr., played pivotal roles in shaping the history we know and live in today. I've had the privilege of writing about some of these icons. Yet, the era was prosperous—prosperous—with many courageous figures like Xernona Clayton, Mrs. Edith Lee Payne, Reverend C.T. Vivian, Reverend Dr. Joseph Lowery, Reverend Dr. Otis Moss, Attorney Fred Gray, Dick Gregory, Elizabeth Eckford, Joan Baez, and many more. Each of them has a unique story that contributed to our collective progress.

I encourage everyone to research the lives and legacies of these remarkable individuals. Through their eyes and experiences, I've gained a deeper understanding of Dr. King, Coretta Scott King, their family, and the movement he led— and perspectives often omitted from history books. As a society, we aren't taught nearly enough about these influential figures and the crucial moments they have shaped. Nor have we been curious enough to understand how they shaped them and the sacrifices it took to stand. It's responsible to actively seek out this knowledge, be inspired by the progress made by others, and use that inspiration to fuel our actions. But I've found that the responsibility lies within us. We must remember that our voices and nonviolent actions hold immense power. That's why it's feared, and mostly, it's by those who resist change.

The lesson that our strength lies in unity is more relevant than ever. Despite ongoing challenges and societal divisions, coming together strengthens us as a community and nation. We are weaker today because division and hate spread like a pervasive disease, weakening the collective strength and unity requisite for a healthy and peaceful society. We are more vulnerable today because we are not educating ourselves. We are weaker today due to our lack of empowering ourselves. We are weaker today because we are fighting, destroying, and killing one another. We are more vulnerable today because of inaction. We are weaker today because they want it that way. These opposing forces create rifts and foster misunderstandings, hindering our ability to effectively work together and address common challenges, making us weak.

Unity in this context is about more than unanimous agreement on every issue. It's about recognizing and respecting our differences while upholding our shared humanity. It's about finding common ground and collaborating toward shared objectives despite having diverse viewpoints and experiences. This approach to unity fosters a society where constructive dialogue and mutual respect prevail, enabling us to achieve collective goals and progress even when we have perceived differences.

This type of dialogue is vital for a thriving society, as it facilitates understanding and helps bridge gaps between different perspectives. By engaging in constructive conversations, we can collaboratively find solutions to complex issues, leading to meaningful progress and positive change.

As history has proven, unity in diversity strengthens society's fabric. It encourages us to look beyond our differences and focus on what we can achieve together for the greater good.

The civil rights movement was a powerful demonstration of individuals from diverse backgrounds, races, and beliefs that challenged and overturned systemic racial injustices. Their unity wasn't based on uniform experiences or opinions but on a shared commitment to fundamental human rights and equality. By focusing on their shared objective rather than their differences, these individual groups created a formidable force against segregation and discrimination. Their strength and collective efforts garnered support from others—across the country. Monumentally, the civil rights movement changed the future of equality in the United States.

This unity was not without loss, pain, challenges, and debates, but the movement's leaders and participants understood that their strength and degree of progress lay in their collective action.

The struggle against hate transcends racial boundaries; it's an individual battle that needs conquering internally. The goal should be to eradicate hate, not perpetuate it. By embracing this mindset and working collectively, we can continue to build a community and a country that is stronger, more compassionate, and inclusive.

Social movements today echo the civil rights movement's spirit, uniting diverse individuals for common causes.

Twenty-five years after my initial visit, I was invited back as the keynote speaker for Fort Bragg's Martin Luther King Jr. celebration. Returning a quarter-century later to embody Dr. King's spirit at this event felt like a momentous full-circle journey. A few years after this memorable occasion, I enthusiastically accepted and was again called upon to speak. As a token of appreciation, I was gifted another beautifully carved wooden statue of Iron Mike, thoughtfully engraved with my name, a cherished memento of these significant experiences.

As a proud Veteran Sergeant of the U.S. Army, having the

opportunity to serve as the keynote speaker for the Sergeants Major Academy Martin Luther King Jr. Celebration was an extraordinary honor. This role was significant, as it brought me back to where my military journey began—a path that spanned four years of dedicated active duty, followed by three years in the reserves. My initial foray into military life started with basic training at Fort Bliss in El Paso, Texas, where I endured the rigorous bivouac in the unforgiving deserts of New Mexico during the peak heat of June, July, and August. Returning to the place that shaped my early military experiences, this time under vastly different circumstances, was a deeply gratifying and full-circle moment. I had seen where the marchers had endured, sacrificed, and marched; I gained a new perspective on what true courage entails. Today's social movements resonate with the spirit of the civil rights movement, bringing together people from various backgrounds to advocate for shared objectives collectively and peacefully.

We have much to do, and there are many unwritten chapters. Today, the loud reverberations of the civil rights movement's call for unity in diversity are still resonating, finding expression in various facets of our society. We see this through the vibrant waves of social movements. These movements draw people from all walks of life, uniting them across racial, socioeconomic, and belief spectra to champion shared objectives, much like the unifying spirit of the civil rights era.

We've witnessed how this principle of inclusivity has also permeated local community engagement. Communities are increasingly coming together, regardless of their diverse backgrounds, to address local issues, organize events, and support local businesses. This collaboration reflects a growing commitment to inclusivity and collective action.

Diversity and inclusion have become more than words; they are integral to company cultures. Businesses actively implement inclusive hiring practices, cultivate diverse work environments, and shape policies that celebrate diversity, recognizing the strength it brings. However, they are not consistent and not enough.

While some education systems are working to remove our history in this wave of change, HBCUs and other education systems have curricula encompassing a broader range of perspectives and histories that foster a more inclusive and comprehensive understanding of society among students.

Political representation gradually reflects this diversity. Policymaking needs to include more individuals from various racial, ethnic, and gender backgrounds, thus ensuring public office and voices and perspectives are represented in policymaking. Yet, we need more individuals with higher integral representation to make decisions on our behalf.

Interfaith and intercultural dialogues are increasing, with increased efforts to build understanding and tolerance among different religious and cultural groups. These dialogues often lead to collaborative efforts to enhance community well-being and promote social justice. We need more acceptance and understanding, or people will lose faith, and generations will be born without it.

The digital age has further amplified the power of unity in diversity. Social media and digital platforms enable diverse groups to connect, mobilize, and raise awareness quickly, sometimes globally, around critical causes and issues. We must use these platforms to support causes, people, and moral and humanitarian initiatives rather than tear people down.

Legal and policy reforms reflect this ongoing journey toward a more equitable society. Efforts continue to address systemic issues, such as police reform, criminal justice reform, and equal rights, but we must be involved. We must actively enforce and implement laws that safeguard the rights and dignity of all human beings.

While making significant strides, the journey toward a fully inclusive and united society remains. Challenges persist, and it requires ongoing dedication and vigilance to maintain and expand upon the principles of unity in diversity. It's a journey that demands our collective effort and commitment, ensuring that the ideals of equality and inclusivity are not just upheld but are lived experiences for everyone. We must ladder up, see what needs to be done and do it.

To honor and perpetuate Dr. Martin Luther King Jr.'s enduring legacy, we must strive to achieve these goals while diligently working to dismantle boundaries and barriers that impede progress. Our approach should embody the peaceful yet resolute spirit that Dr. King championed. As we navigate the complexities of today's society, we must continuously strive to uphold the principles of equality, justice, and nonviolence that he passionately advocated for. In doing so, we will keep his vision alive and contribute to creating a more just and peaceful world.

*When you know the facts
and have the truth in your hands,
you can't help but learn.*

-from the chapter An Ordinary Man's Extraordinary Faith

TheDreamLives.com

You would think you were listening to a recording of Dr. Martin Luther King Jr. speaking. Some even say Reverend Stephon Ferguson channels the spirit of Dr. King. Among them are members of King's family who say Ferguson sounds closer to MLK than anyone they've ever heard recite his words.

From the pulpit of historic Ebenezer Baptist Church in Atlanta, Georgia to Teatro Lope de Vega in Madrid, Spain, Ferguson has traveled across the US and internationally, performing as one of the greatest leaders in the history of the world. He breathes life into the words of Dr. King, captivating people of all ages, cultures, and backgrounds by delivering dead-on, pitch-perfect renditions. Ferguson has memorized and delivered most of Dr. King's most memorable speeches and sermons with the same passion. His mission is to help continue the legacy of Dr. King by reciting King's words and, more importantly, educating people about his philosophy of love, peace, and equality to help bring about positive change. Born in Albany, New York, Ferguson is a native of Fayetteville, NC. He served as a Sergeant Medic in the U.S. Army and later worked as a radio personality and news reporter. He served in the ministry at Simon Temple AME Zion Church in Fayetteville, NC. Ferguson moved to Atlanta, Georgia in the spring of 2011 where he served as an Associate Minister at the historic Greater Piney Grove Baptist Church in Atlanta.

In Atlanta, Ferguson worked closely with the MLK National Historical Park at Ebenezer Baptist Church, King's home church, where he gave historical presentations and reenactments and educated people on the history of the church and Dr. King. Dr. Ferguson is certified by The King Center and Emory University to teach the Kingian Nonviolence Curriculum and is Certified Level II & III by the University of Rhode Island's Center for Nonviolence & Peace Studies. He has completed courses on the life of Dr. King at Morehouse School of Religion at ITC and Stanford University.

Below are leaders who have heard Ferguson and their testimonies. Visit TheDreamLives.com for more information about his work.

"You know they usually play a tape of Dr. King's speeches and sermons. So, I'm hearing this and I'm looking for the tape machine...only to find that Stephon Ferguson is the machine. He sounds just like him!"
-**Rev. Jesse Jackson,** Rainbow PUSH

"You come at a good time. 50% of the people living in the United States today were not born when King was assassinated. So, when they hear you, they're hearing Dr. King for the first time and that's very important."
- **Dick Gregory,** Activist, Comedian

Following a performance of the I Have a Dream speech in Atlanta, GA – *"You got it! You got Him (Dr. King) down pat. I felt it when you were delivering it. You got it!"*
– **John Lewis,** Congressman

"Very, very strong! Very powerful! I'm inspired by hearing you in the spirit of Dr. King. And the fact that you have the speeches memorized like that—very lengthy speeches—says a great deal about the admiration and respect you have for him!"
- **Tyrese Gibson,** Actor, Recording Artist

"I don't think I've heard it that well besides from the recording of Dr. King himself. It was truly like hearing history reborn."
– **Beverly Perdue,** NC Governor

"I have heard many renditions of Dr. Martin Luther King Jr., but never have I heard one as powerful and as moving as the rendition Stephon Ferguson delivers."
– **Marshall Pitts, Jr.,** Mayor Fayetteville NC

"God has truly given him the gift of bringing out Dr. King's words and reminding us of how personal his words are to us, and leaving us with a voice in our head, even today, that tells us there's still a lot of work to be done."
– **Judy Forte,** MLK NHP Superintendent

"As Mr. Ferguson's eloquent voice resonated throughout the auditorium, one could easily mistake his oratory as a recording of Dr. King's inspiring delivery. He is truly a gifted artist whose talents enrich the lives of others."
- **Dr. TJ Bryan,** Chancellor Fayetteville State University

Media Features:

TIME Magazine MARCH 02, 2020, Issue / Atlanta Magazine / ABC News / CNN's Great Big Story / CSPAN / The Atlanta Voice / 400 YAAHC / Tom Joyner Morning Show / The Fayetteville Observer / The Fayetteville Press / WBS Channel 2 Atlanta / WABE NPR News / Omaha World-Herald / Baltimore Sun / The National SCLC Magazine / Deutsche Welle (German International) / WTVD 11 ABC / CBSN Chicago / WREG (CBS) Memphis TN / CBS 6 Richmond, VA....

Education:

Doctor of Ministry (Summa Cum Laude)
Morehouse School of Religion @ ITC
Master of Divinity (Cum Laude)
Morehouse School of Religion @ ITC
Master of Ministry (Summa Cum Laude) Andersonville Theological Seminary

Bachelor of Arts. Communications and Media. (Summa Cum Laude) Fayetteville State University
Bachelor of Biblical Studies. AMES Christian University
Associate of Arts. Film Georgia State University
Associate of Arts. Theatre. Georgia Perimeter College

Acknowledgments

The Late Rev. Dr. Richard Cobble
Omega Holiness Church Family in Atlanta, GA.
Dr. Themba Mafico
Professor and advisor, for his wisdom and guidance.
Everett and Glenda Smith for their great friendship and support.
Wes & Sandy Cookman & the WIDU Family in Fayetteville, NC.
Dr. Mark Thompson - Redemptive Life Christian Fellowship.

About the Author

Stephon Ferguson is widely recognized for his exceptional ability to embody the voice and spirit of Martin Luther King, Jr., and in "Legacy Reloaded; A Nonviolent Awakening," he brings that same passion and authenticity to his writing. Through vivid storytelling and compelling analysis, Ferguson draws from the wisdom of Martin Luther King, Jr., and sheds light on the often-overlooked influence of Nonviolence in shaping the course of history, making a compelling case for its enduring significance.

"Legacy Reloaded; A Nonviolent Awakening" is a timely and essential read for individuals seeking to understand and engage in the ongoing struggle for a more just and equitable society. With its powerful message of hope and unity, this book is poised to inspire and empower readers from all walks of life.

Made in the USA
Columbia, SC
02 March 2025

54607405R00100